JUN 4 2001

EAST MEADOW PUBLIC LIBRARY

3 1299 00621 7104

The Great Gatsby and Fitzgerald's World of Ideas

D1197002

JUN 4 2001

THE GREAT GATSBY

and Fitzgerald's World of Ideas

Ronald Berman

THE UNIVERSITY OF ALABAMA PRESS

Tuscaloosa and London

Copyright © 1997
THE UNIVERSITY OF ALABAMA PRESS
Tuscaloosa, Alabama 35487-0380
All rights reserved
Manufactured in the United States of America

Quotations from *The Great Gatsby* are reprinted by permission of Scribner, a
Division of Simon & Schuster, from the Authorized Text Edition of *The Great
Gatsby* by F. Scott Fitzgerald. Edited by Matthew J. Bruccoli. Copyright 1925 by
Charles Scribner's Sons. Copyright © 1991, 1992 by Eleanor Lanahan, Matthew J.
Bruccoli, and Samuel J. Lanahan as Trustees under Agreement dated 7/3/75,
created by Frances Scott Fitzgerald Smith.

∞

The paper on which this book is printed meets the minimum requirements
of American National Standard for Information Science–Permanence of
Paper for Printed Library Materials, ANSI Z39.48-1984.

Library of Congress Cataloging-in-Publication Data

Berman, Ronald.
The Great Gatsby and Fitzgerald's world of ideas / Ronald Berman.
p.   cm.
Includes bibliographical references and index.
ISBN 0-8173-1073-8 (alk. paper)
1. Fitzgerald, F. Scott (Francis Scott), 1896–1940.   Great Gatsby.
2. Fitzgerald, F. Scott (Francis Scott), 1896–1940—Political and social
views.   3. Fitzgerald, F. Scott (Francis Scott), 1896–1940—Philosophy.
4. Literature and society—United States—History—20th century.
5. Social values in literature.   6. Philosophy in literature.   I. Title.
PS3511.I9G823   1997
813'.52—dc21   96-45287

British Library Cataloguing-in-Publication Data available

1   2   3   4   5   •   04   03   02   01   00

For Rich Ekman

You say: "The story is fundamentally trivial." I think the smooth, almost unbroken pattern makes you feel that. Despite your admiration for Conrad you have lately—perhaps in reaction against the merely well-made novels of James' imitators—become used to the formless.

—FSF to H. L. Mencken, May 1925

If my novel is an anecdote so is *The Brothers Karamazoff.*

—FSF to Edmund Wilson, May 1925

CONTENTS

Acknowledgments   xi

Introduction   1

1. Old Values and New Times   18
2. Demos   44
3. Community and Crowd   68
4. Mixed Democracy   89
5. Individualism Reconsidered   110
6. Energies   131
7. Belief and Will   155
8. Ruins and Order   175

Notes   201

Bibliography   219

Index   227

ACKNOWLEDGMENTS

Research into the first quarter of this century reminds us how much there is to read about the collision of traditional and modern ideas and especially about the debate over social philosophies. I am grateful to the research libraries of the University of California, which have provided access to the books, magazines, and newspapers of a period vanishing quickly into the past. Milton R. Stern has provided important critical readings and advice. Among scholars, I am especially grateful to Matthew J. Bruccoli, who has been the first reader of this text and who has made it more accurate than it would otherwise have been. It would not have been possible to work on Fitzgerald's text or letters or life without reliance on Professor Bruccoli's lifetime of scholarship.

Passages from *The Great Gatsby* are without exception quoted from the Cambridge edition cited in the bibliography, reprinted by permission of Scribner, a Division of Simon & Schuster, from the Authorized Text Edition of *The Great Gatsby* by F. Scott Fitzgerald, edited by Matthew J. Bruccoli, Copyright 1925 by Charles Scribner's Sons, Copyright © 1991, 1992 by Eleanor Lanahan, Matthew J. Bruccoli, and Samuel J. Lanahan as Trustees under Agreement dated 7/3/75, created by Frances Scott Fitzgerald Smith. Page numbers are provided parenthetically in the text.

The University of Alabama Press deserves more praise than I can easily state. I thank Nicole Mitchell, director and editor-in-chief, and the staff of the University Press, who have worked far beyond the call of duty. And, I could not have edited this manuscript without Barbara, Kathy, and Julie Berman.

The Great Gatsby and Fitzgerald's World of Ideas

INTRODUCTION

For most of his professional life, F. Scott Fitzgerald was deeply aware of the conflict between modern times and what he called, in 1937, "the old America."[1] Sometimes that older nation appears in his work, as in "The Diamond As Big as the Ritz," self-evidently ready for renewal or for destruction. It is a world of excess and pretense, with a special morality of wealth. Like many other Americans, Fitzgerald called the prewar past Victorian, and like them, he no longer felt bound by its imperatives. But that world will also be viewed, as Charlie Wales recalls it in "Babylon Revisited," as at least a point of certainty—if it were only possible morally and intellectually to "jump back a whole generation."[2] The major figures of *The Great Gatsby* are located between those two American worlds.

Like "The Diamond As Big as the Ritz," *The Great*

Gatsby plainly implies that the morals, ideas, and ideals of old America cannot and should not last into modern times. But it longs for certainties that have been displaced without being replaced.

The scholarship on this novel has concentrated on critical interpretation, but there are many sources of both old and new material. It is important to bear in mind Fitzgerald's own recollections of issues of the first quarter of the twentieth century and the ways they appeared in the literary marketplace. I have tried to identify and describe certain arguments and problems stated by the text and to connect the specific language used with the language of national debate. In all cases I have tried to compare Fitzgerald's prose with the examination of American life in the first quarter of the twentieth century. And I have concentrated on firsthand cultural and intellectual sources rather than cover ground already made familiar by the critics of this novel. Much of the material I have used comes from sources other than novelists and critics of the twenties. Of course, writers like H. L. Mencken and Edmund Wilson have been invaluable—but a number of people outside the field had literature on their minds.

One thing that I have found is that Fitzgerald was a first-rate observer of the American scene. It is, I think, no longer possible to think of him as a lightweight; he was, in fact, more knowledgeable and considerably more sensible than those who have confused his life with his mind. We may not find in *The Great Gatsby* issues that dominate debate now, at our end of the century; there is no use looking for them. What we will find is the structuring of a narrative around the idea of democracy in 1922. And that took place on the terrain of another country.

The more *The Great Gatsby* recedes into the historical distance, the easier it becomes to lose sight of the differences between then and now. We begin to use a critical terminology—often centering on our own ideas of what is "moral" or "democratic"—that does not register changes of meaning. Many ideas and many texts with time-bound meanings are refracted in Fitzgerald's text. We ought to be aware of the language that he elects to repeat, of the issues he introduces (often from both sides of the argument), and of the ways in which the ideas he presents differ from their current forms. Below are three cross-cutting ways in which I have tried to organize subjects within my chapters.

Transvaluations

The language of *The Great Gatsby* includes certain words that studies of imagery are bound to ignore. They have little poetic valency; and they are in some sense invisible. But these fairly commonplace words have changed their meanings considerably in the three generations since Fitzgerald used them. And even when they were first applied in the text of his novel, they were to be taken in a special sense by his first readers. The reason was a long and sustained debate then underway about American social and personal meanings.

The debate involved books, magazines—even the fiction of Fitzgerald, who as early as *Flappers and Philosophers* echoed some of its issues. In "Head and Shoulders" (1920) he has Horace Tarbox, an equivocal hero but an interestingly literate man, wondering whether to begin "his series of essays on 'The Pragmatic Bias of the New Realists.' "[3] At a later point in the story Horace announces that his "chief interest in life is the study of modern philosophy." Neither Horace nor Fitzgerald seems to know much about the details, but characteristically they are both familiar with the outlines: nothing can be more plausible than another project of Horace Tarbox to "popularize" or do for realist philosophy what William James has already done for "pragmatism." Such popularization is occurring all around Horace in the literary marketplace as philosophy turns toward social issues. In fact, at roughly the same time that he appears in print, another Fitzgerald figure, Amory Blaine, is debating the idea of "leaders" of society in a way that echoes dependence not only on the James of "Great Men and Their Environment" but Santayana, who spoke of the need for "natural leaders" to serve an unwilling democracy.[4] From the beginning, Fitzgerald had a keen ear for readers' views on public issues and especially for their doubts about the link between American ideas and American realities.

Some of the words that Fitzgerald later uses in *The Great Gatsby,* like "family" and "home," seem to have fairly continuous meanings. But their use in the text suggests that a process of redefinition has already begun. They are words common to the Public Philosophy that rested on the work of William James, words used with great frequency both just before and during the twenties. When Tom Buchanan invokes some of these words, like "family," are we intended to see the extended late Victorian family? Or do we refer ourselves to its modern and attenuated form? Do we force the phrase (as I think we should do) to operate under the burden of diminution of its traditional powers, even the threat of its dissolution, and other particularized meanings? Other words appear to be even more simple, but they will cause us much more difficulty: "I" and "we" refer to American selves, and the identity of those selves is not what it is now and certainly not what it was just before Fitzgerald's invocation of them. When Daisy says "I" in the novel, does she mean her social, representative (and other-directed) self or rather a newly subjective and altogether morally harder person?

Especially under the influence of that Public Philosophy of the first quarter of the century, a whole realm of evidently familiar words and ideas and allegiances came in for reexamination. I have tried to look at words that have something to do with the language of *The Great Gatsby* and certainly those that are central and sometimes conflictual in it. Here, for example, is what Josiah Royce thought it necessary to say about one familiar category:

> While you can never be loyal to what you take to be a merely abstract principle, nevertheless, it is equally true that you can never be genuinely loyal merely to an individual human being, taken just as this detached creature. You can, indeed, love your friend, viewed just as this individual. But love for an individual is so far just a fondness for a fascinating human presence. . . . You can be, and should be, loyal to your friendship.[5]

It may seem a surprise to have a thinker of Royce's standing talk in such sermonical terms and about such self-evident ideas, but the title of his book is in part an explanation: he writes with the assurance that his title— *William James and Other Essays on the Philosophy of Life*—is in fact self-evident. He knows that throughout the literary marketplace, in a changing society, people are aware of new meanings in the most basic relationships and of writings about them. Others—for example, Santayana and John Dewey—wrote the same kinds of essays, with the same references to James, who was at the center of the Public Philosophy. James himself, Dewey, Santayana, Royce, and others like Walter Lippmann tried to recreate for their time the meaning of social existence in America. They spent a great deal of time on language and had much to say about the relationship of philosophy, poetry, and the novel.

I will try to show how specific ideas and words found their expression in Public Philosophy, and why they migrated to other texts, including Fitzgerald's. He echoes a great American conversation throughout his lifetime, from one end to the other: William James was writing about problems of democratic life before 1896, and John Dewey was responding to his views after 1940.

There are themes and even plots in the background: Santayana's *The Life of Reason* contains eight chapters, six of which find echoes in literature at large and in Fitzgerald's text. These concern love, the family, the aristocratic ideal, democracy, free society, and ideal society—and their decline. It might take a fairly long book to trace just a few of these ideas from the century's end to their redefinition (or dissolution) under modernism. But clearly Fitzgerald's text takes up the ideas and ideology of some of these headings. In *The Culture of Time and Space, 1880–1918*, Stephen Kern cites the early Lippmann on changes in the common understanding of "the sanctity of property, the patriarchal family, hereditary caste," none of which any longer held an absolute connotation.[6] Or a moral imperative. To return to Santayana, we might note the subject of the aristocratic ideal. It was of especial interest because it had been put into play by James, who was so conscious of the loss of American "patrician" leadership in modern times. Debate would be continued by Lippmann during the twenties, in his forcible writings about the end of *any* visible leadership in the postwar decade. Does Tom Buchanan fit into a discussion of this sort? Does Nick Carraway have meaningful opinions on such issues?

The Great Gatsby asks many questions within the terminology of Public Philosophy. It asks, if implicitly, what is the good life? It sets up for us governing ideas on loyalty, friendship, married and unmarried love, family, self, and "home." Its questions are sometimes highly explicit, especially when we are asked to think about conflicts between values and about the relationship of values to acts. The major figures of this novel are often asked to do the same. The book begins with a statement of tolerance, but I don't think it is a tolerant book, although it is an understanding one. We ought to recognize that it was written at a time and about a time when language was deeply moralized.

On Democratic Character

Certain issues addressed by *The Great Gatsby* are visible in American intellectual life and in the life of mass media whose business it is to echo ideas. These issues center on the slippery social character of democracy. For example, in a series of essays that ran from 1920 to 1927, H. L. Mencken queried the nature of democracy and stated what he thought were some of its current problems. He formulated one issue central to Fitzgerald's writing: "the plutocracy, in a democratic state, tends inevitably . . . to take the place of the missing aristocracy and even to be mistaken for it. It is, of course, something quite different. It lacks all the essential characters of a true aristocracy: a clean tradition, culture, public spirit, honesty, honor, courage—above all courage."[7] Mencken has captured the sense of opposition between individuals and groups of the early twenties, but what seemed simple to Mencken and to other editorialists became more complex in novelistic form. Clearly, Fitzgerald was interested by what Mencken called "the missing aristocracy," but he was even more concerned with the way that character evolved from ideas. In *The Great Gatsby* we see two characters framed by this debate, Gatsby, who relies on money and tries to forget his origins, and Tom Buchanan, who mistakes each and every one of the class values from "tradition" to "courage" summarized by Mencken. But their relationship to ideas has, of course, been reversed, the work of the novel being to complicate formulations and to show how character is related to idea and is created by idea.

Walter Lippmann stated a second mutual issue about the times in 1929: "What most distinguishes the generation who have approached maturity since the debacle of idealism at the end of the War is not their rebellion against the religion and the moral code of their parents, but their disillusionment with their own rebellion."[8] Fitzgerald has pointedly set up an opposition between generations in *The Great Gatsby,* and those who are old in this story suffer more than the usual liabilities of age. Meyer Wolfsheim sentimentally knows that he belongs in the past; Dan Cody (in one aspect of his persona) represents the dead hand of Victorian egotism. But most of the problems of the generation who make up the cast of major characters are problems of the present moment, and problems that have been self-generated. Although the narrative begins with an evocation of tolerance, by its end moral judgments available only from the past can be applied.

A third issue: when Fitzgerald uses certain phrases, for example "vitality," and when he describes certain phenomena, for example, the indistinguishable crowd, he takes his definitions from particular debates on national character. The vital individual is a kind of hero (or heroine) of democratic life, a source of the "energy" that makes society work and advances it.[9] But the mindless crowd is what democratic society can become when values are abandoned. The text of *The Great Gatsby* persistently examines individuals in terms of the vitality they bring to their ideas, and it senses social order—and disorder—in the groups and swarms and crowds who make up the background of the story. Again, Fitzgerald complicates issues: he admires vitality while realizing that it may be uncontrollable, and he admires the urgency of self-expression and of social change while realizing that they may take us where we should not go.

When we see and hear Myrtle Wilson we encounter a specifically democratic sensibility, more complex than it appears:

> "My dear," she cried, "I'm going to give you this dress as soon as I'm through with it. I've got to get another one tomorrow. I'm going to make a list of all the things I've got to get. A massage and a wave and a collar for the dog and one of those cute little ash trays where you touch a spring, and a wreath with a black silk bow for mother's grave that'll last all summer. I got to write down a list so I won't forget all the things I got to do." [31][10]

The things that Myrtle wants to buy are of course identical with the things she wants to "do." The words "get" and "got" make up a huge part of her operational language. The content of her dream is quite precise: she is not upscale and has no plans for attacking Fifth Avenue. Myrtle thinks in terms of ads and dime-store inventory: a diamond doesn't need a list. What she says releases a gram of the information on her mind, a brief burst of commodities and purposes that exist in a kind of precompositional sincerity. Is she simply materialistic? It would be easy to dismiss her on that ground, but Myrtle's imagination is worth knowing. She is a figure not only of this novel but of American philosophical inquiry. This torrent of language and desire adds up to a vision of self already apparent to James and especially to Santayana:

> The American is imaginative; for where life is intense, imagination is intense also. Were he not imaginative he would not live so much in the future. But his imagination is practical, and the future it forecasts is immediate; it works with the clearest and least ambiguous terms known to his experience. . . . There is an enthusiasm in his sympathetic handling of material forces which goes far to cancel the illiberal character which it might otherwise assume.[11]

I think the last covers Myrtle Wilson, for women as well as men had in the early twenties begun to share the ambitions of change. The statement certainly covers Fitzgerald himself, because as the country began its goodbye to the past he became deeply sympathetic to "the movement of a vast, seething, progressive society."[12] Fitzgerald caught the energy of this social maelstrom, and the language of his fiction depicts its release.

Promise Versus Possibility

The first chapter of *The Great Gatsby* does not tell us where we are going. It raises many subjects, and part of the problem of reading the text is finding the connection between episodes and between dialogues. One thing this chapter does accomplish is to set the narrative firmly in a certain place, historical America after two wars. Its problems are certainly universal human problems—but they are also specifically American. This chapter creates a context of breakdown. I am not referring only to the way the evening at the Buchanans' proceeds; certain American ideas are stated, allegiances to them are declared—while what happens undermines both actions and ideas. The technique is more than satirical because we are left with serious doubts not only about the people we see but about traditional ways of understanding them.

We don't meet the protagonist for a long time, about a quarter of the way into the story. Until we do meet him, there is elaborate description of his context. At the Buchanans' and at Myrtle Wilson's New York apartment, dialogue refers almost continuously to American selves. Characters have a great deal to say about how they view themselves; what they want in life; even what they think of current ideas and institutions. All are engaged by the promise of American life—yet all must deal with its limiting contradictions. Above all, there are issues of stasis and change, the latter ranging from its earthly and comic form of social mobility to the myth of metamorphosis. In 1922, Myrtle Wilson and Molly Bloom have some of the same things on their mind and share the "endless creativity of . . . present consciousness" about themselves and their selves.[13]

When we do meet Gatsby, after having glimpsed him through others, we do not get all the information usually provided about novelistic character. We can sense that his character will and must have something to do with the context that has been set. The narrative then accrues information about him, but a good percentage of this is false information. Yet something essential for our understanding of the text takes place, and that is the development of an idea about Gatsby. We read first of a man whose character is different, even mysterious. We are less interested in his character than in his situation because we have been guided by figures in both foreground and background of the story. But Gatsby moves ever closer to the center.

Because Fitzgerald is so skilled, the narrative seems like a reasonably disorderly recollection, inconsistent but true. But the sequence of chapters is very important because particular arguments are being advanced. Each chapter extends argument. As Harry Levin wrote of *Madame Bovary,* each individual chapter becomes a "clear-cut designation" of time and place, hence of certain governing ideas.[14] I have necessarily followed the chapter sequence of *The Great Gatsby* because the release of information by the text is so calculated. My own chapters will follow the novel's organization.

Fitzgerald's text begins by telling us about Gatsby's restlessness. In the early twenties restlessness was thought to be peculiarly American, equally a necessity and a virtue signifying individualist dissatisfaction with the way things were and incentive to improve them. Also important to conceptions of Americanism is the next information of its kind released by the text, that Gatsby has a certain kind of energy, the "vitality" that I have mentioned, often adduced as an essential part of national character. The phrase rebounds in American writing before and during the twenties, an essential in ideas of national psychology and even of politics. As I've noted, it has moral connotations, being widely understood to be the ground structure of moral consciousness. Without "energy" or "vitality" there could be no will, hence no heroism of act or belief. But it was also understood that vital personality had to navigate through the dangers of individualism and subjectivity.

Gatsby's mental energy is the more noticeable because it is displayed in a world of entropy. Those around him do not wish to be awakened into consciousness, and the text has a very large vocabulary of tedium, exhaustion, indecision, and passivity of will—even of paralysis of will. These were qualities perceived in "civilized" American life by William James, who applauded the work of imagination in dispelling them. These inert qualities may even be said, in James's view, to dominate that life. *The Great Gatsby,* like the aggregate of James's works, is infiltrated by the language of moral decision, which is exerted in opposition to those qualities. In many ways Fitzgerald remained faithful to the Jamesian ideas on his horizon. He certainly was part of the evolving tradition of commenting on those ideas.

As the story progresses, the theory of Gatsby proceeds: he not only becomes more of an individual, he becomes more of an individual than anyone else in the book. He reveals certain attitudes about himself, and Nick Carraway makes some important connections between them and national character. We find that Gatsby has constructed himself from books and magazines, within certain implications. We find that ideas of romance, success, and honor matter a great deal, and stay with him. The idea of being a "great man" is introduced into the text, and we are invited to think about the way this important phrase has reverberated throughout Gatsby's lifetime—and Fitzgerald's. Great men are, after all, public figures, and the essence of their greatness is widely understood to be its representative, national quality. The title of the novel should suggest that. With Gatsby, we begin with an idea of difference, proceed to an idea about moral energy, detect a kind of individualism, and finally begin to understand its heroic quality and its American context. We want to remember that Fitzgerald's alternative title for *The Great Gatsby* was *Under the Red, White, and Blue.* This shadow title has many implications for personal and national lives. How, in the early twenties, did values convey themselves, and how were they to be interpreted? How, under this flag, do we make sense of the fleeting moment and the evanescence of ideas?

◪ 1 ◪

Old Values and New Times

T*he Great Gatsby* is a post-war book, but I think most readers have the wrong war in mind. The moral exhaustion we detect in character and language is historical and literary. It does not proceed directly from the culture-shattering First World War, although some excellent recent books have shown us how serious was the effect of that war on feeling and idea.[1] Fitzgerald thought intelligently about social change and in an interview during January 1921 spoke about it in the following way:

> I am tired, too, of hearing that the world war broke down the moral barriers of the younger generation. Indeed, except for leaving its touch of destruction here and there, I do not think the war left any real lasting effect. Why, it is almost forgotten right now.

18

The younger generation has been changing all thru the last twenty years. The war had little or nothing to do with it. I put the change up to literature. Our skepticism or cynicism, if you wish to call it that, or, if you are older, our callow flippancy, is due to the way H. G. Wells and other intellectual leaders have been thinking and reflecting life.[2]

He put the character of the cultural moment into a single clause, "radical departures from the Victorian era." Too much weight should not be borne by one statement, but we ought to pursue its theme in search of more evidence.

The emphasis of the novel's opening pages is post–Civil War, on "three generations" of fathers and uncles and sons. The Carraway family, fittingly for this story, has been steadily upwardly mobile. The Civil War began its prosperity; the Gilded Age confirmed it. By the third generation Nick has gone to Yale and to easy association with millionaires. It has been a family decision to send Nick back east—aunts, uncles, and father are involved, and some are even implicated in his story. Especially the "hard-boiled" uncle who seems to have been the first cause of the family's rise to prosperity. His brief biography is the first in *The Great Gatsby*'s spectrum of American lives. We will get a great deal of information from these lives, and they will offer thematic parallels to the main story. This particular biography gives us a necessary sense of unheroic American realities, of the relationship of money to all else. And of the falsifications of history.

The references back across the generations to the commercially satisfying Civil War set both protagonist and reader in "the Victorian era." But something has happened: the unregenerate uncle may look forever out of his painting with the same wise brutality that made for his success, but the world of his assumptions is gone. Three generations ago, in the beginning, there was no nonsense about ideas or identities. But both Middle West and family have lost their initiative. They are what one leaves behind for a stronger source of energy. The first page of the novel is in fact about kinds of energy; and its calculated diminishment tells us that "the Victorian era" has little any longer to give or to command. *The Great Gatsby* begins with a hesitant and rather loose-jointed account of what a nineteenth-century father passes on to his twentieth-century son. The narration is inarticulate, suggesting the deficiencies of content through those of form. We expect greater things but hear only polite fictions about family, class, and "clan." Expecting revelations, we hear of decencies: the text establishes the virtues of reserve, tolerance, and of an idealized self-consciousness that seems to be nothing more than the suppression of impulse.

The story has begun with the invocation of the sacred subjects of life and literature from Scott through Stevenson: war and peace, family, "tradition," and "clan." We expect the hero to have something to say in relation to them. We also expect him to begin his journey with some talisman that these great subjects provide. But the narration gives us nothing that will guard against danger. This particular story about seeking your fortune begins with an ended moment.[3]

There is a tremendous upsurge of energy (literally, as in the description of Gatsby and the seismograph) when we move away from outmoded sources and toward money, sex, and self-fashioning. There are in fact talismans for some of these things, "shining secrets" (7) that show us the way. With their mention the narrative changes and becomes full of color and movement. But we don't at this point suspect the powers of refiguration of money or sexuality.

In New York and on West Egg, Nick (correctly) perceives character, statement, and idea in terms of dubiety and opposition. He recalls facts while establishing uncertainties and even anxieties about them. We are constrained by the text to the visual but in terms of its limits: "perpetual confusion . . . factual imitation . . . overlooked . . . I had no sight. . . . appearance . . . impression." Enormous power is diffused into ungoverned motion through a language of "anticlimax" and, repeatedly, "drift."[4] A kind of principle of uncertainty is being elaborated that will extend from the use of language to the nature of identity, historical and otherwise.

Uncertainty will be restated in many forms. The

story has begun by invoking "the abnormal mind" as against that of "a normal person" (5). However, characters (Tom, Myrtle, Catherine) will think routinely of being "crazy" as an explanation of feeling. Dan Cody will be described as on and then over the "verge of softmindedness" (78), like the brewer who liked roofs thatched with straw. Tom believes in "science" but also in "a second sight" (95) that tells him what to do. Jordan is sexually attractive in part because of her moral and stylistic deviance. Drunkenness, throughout, is a form of revelatory unconsciousness, an enormous part of the telling of the story. Dreams demand their interpretation—and had since 1900 demanded *The Interpretation of Dreams*.[5] On one level this is all convincing context—in 1925 Franklin P. Adams and Brian Hooker collaborated on music and lyrics of "Don't Tell Me What You Dreamed Last Night (For I've Been Reading Freud)."[6] Everyone who reads in 1925 knows about sex and the unconscious mind. But the biggest dream in the text will never be explained by therapy. Explanation comes easily and often in this text but is rarely useful.

More uncertainty: the conventional language of description seems not to matter to the narrator. We don't know what Daisy looks like. Nick is never described. Jordan exists in terms of style and form and attitude. People "resemble" things: Daisy and her daughter, Gatsby and that "advertisement."

There is, however, much hidden information, as when Fitzgerald forcibly directs our attention to lyrics that are on Daisy's mind: "I looked outdoors for a minute and it's very romantic outdoors. There's a bird on the lawn that I think must be a nightingale come over on the Cunard or White Star Line" (16). According to the notes in Matthew J. Bruccoli's edition, "there are no nightingales in the United States" (183). Fitzgerald repeats the word "romantic" three times in a very short burst of dialogue to redirect us. In Keats and Shelley (and later in Eliot), the nightingale awakens dead souls from "dull oblivion."[7] The process, Eliot reminds us, is unwilling, and the nightingale's song is unheard by most. The subject of entropy resurfaces often in contemporary reflections on a national life of complacency and moral inertia, and I will return to this point.

When Daisy speaks and is described, certain words enforce attention. The reader who overlooks "promise" and "promising" will miss their connection to the restatement of "promise" in the narration. Even more, the reader will miss the meaning of the phrase in its time as a synonym for American dreaming. It is a phrase often applied to the idea of the nation. And it is linked, in essays and magazines and political visions, to "reward" and to "progress." *Vanity Fair,* for example begins each issue with the hope that it has recorded "the progress and promise of American life." And in 1922, the *Saturday Evening Post* is one of many voices linking success to life in "a land of promise."[8] To be sure, her voice is full of money if it is full of promise.

When we first meet Daisy and Jordan, we are asked

to think of subjectivity and theatricality: she and Jordan look "as though upon an anchored balloon" and "as if" they had just been blown back after a flight around the house; Jordan looks "as if" she were balancing something, and Daisy laughs "as if" she had said something witty (10–11). One of Daisy's lies is in this mode: "She was only extemporizing but a stirring warmth flowed from her as if her heart was trying to come out to you concealed in one of those breathless, thrilling words" (15). "As if," a kind of false subjunctive, is connected firmly to "concealed . . . words." Display and concealment will often be linked in the text and by no means only in the case of Jay Gatsby.

Much of what Nick discovers is the opposite of what he sees, hears, or is assured. Even among the banalities of introduction he can sense the difference between gesture and fact, speech and sensibility. In half a sentence— "If she saw me out of the corner of her eyes she gave no hint of it" (10)—there are complications of time, probability, intention, sincerity, display, concealment, and perception: does Jordan see him or ignore him? If the first, does that have something to do with the way she sees anything? Is her silence an expression of character or a form of female strategy? Her self-possession and unself-consciousness are a contrast to Daisy's expressiveness and reliance on sound and movement. Are these complicating and supporting female roles? As Marjorie tells us in "Bernice Bobs Her Hair," even sixteen-year-olds have a "line."

Tom shows effeminate swank and Jordan looks like "a young cadet" (12). Nick says a lot of interesting things—things that might become interesting—but he keeps them to himself. They do not become dialogue, so that they hang in the air as a secondary set of subjects shadowing those things that are stated and argued. For this reason the novel has both a surface and uncharted depth. The style of modernism conjoins the sexes, but we may be intended to sense here Jordan's probing of boundaries, her own readiness, in a novel of identities, to assume a character.[9]

There are many telephone calls in the novel, like the one that interrupts Tom's following lecture to Daisy, Jordan, and Nick on "science and art and all that" (14). The "shrill metallic urgency" (16) of these calls suggests information to be revealed and truths necessary to the understanding of events. The telephone suggests not only reality but realism. But any sense we have of communicability, hence of actuality, coexists with a highly indeterminate dialogue: *The Great Gatsby* depends to an enormous degree on the communication of lies, fictions, and misinformation. For example, what Nick has learned at Yale has to be revised and abandoned.[10] What he hears from Daisy is a social fiction: "This was a permanent move, said Daisy over the telephone, but I didn't believe it" (9). The Buchanans are old friends scarcely known at all; Nick is described as a rose but knows that he is "not even faintly like" one (15); Daisy's explanations reveal "basic insincerity" (17); the word "secret" is repeated a number of times, finally suggesting that even "turbulent emotions" do not find honest expression. The word "sophisticated" means holding off truth. "But we heard it," Daisy says of Nick's nonexistent engagement. Fitzgerald introduces into the text gossip, rumor, and "story," giving us to understand that they become part of both narrative and character private and public. The idea of "story" itself is deeply affected.

I have argued for a sense of difficulty in interpreting the language of the text, which means a modification of literary method. The following critical advice is helpful but only to a certain extent:

> Fitzgerald took literary impressionism—with its emphasis on the incremental impressions of light falling upon the eye of a single limited observer fixed in time and place—toward its extreme limits. He eliminated almost all images of sound, touch, taste, and smell in favor of images of the eye and then restricted these almost entirely to visions of 1) motion and stillness, 2) light and darkness, and 3) the primary colors.[11]

But Fitzgerald has also limited "images of the eye." What is visual in this text is often also indiscernible. And it is simply not enough to determine kinds of imagery: the text is insistent in its statement of terms that counteract the perception and the understanding of "images." The first chapter warns us that "words" deceive, that meaning is "concealed," that "concentration" falters, that "meaning" is hard to ascertain, that the evening described has dissolved into "broken fragments" (16). The text is itself a collection of fragments. It is not really possible to construct imagistic certainties from a text that denies the capacity rightly to conceive, perceive, or conclude.

One of the great conflicts in the novel's opening chapter is literary-textual, between the values of realism and the complexities that cannot be expressed or understood by conventional description. Nick does not fully see or understand what he perceives, and neither do we. Dialogue resists analysis because so much of its motivation is suspect and so much of its statement untrue. As Nick states of one moment, what he overhears is only "on the verge of coherence" (15). Description uncontaminated by dialogue repeatedly *denotes* perceptual uncertainty. It may be that "a certain hardy skepticism" (16) is called for, which is to say, the ability to see through things as they are, because they are not what they seem to be. (Jordan, without dreams, has the right kind of mind for this world.) The use of weighted summary phrases that establish conclusions reached by Nick at the end of episodes ("confused," "basic insincerity," "trick," "untrue," "I couldn't guess what Daisy and Tom were thinking)" (16) establishes the limits of our knowledge because of the limits of perception. The admonition from Tom to Nick toward chapter's end is really from narrator to reader: "Don't believe everything you hear" (19).

Some ideas and assumptions came to Fitzgerald from other texts—he was himself indefatigable in pointing out the "influences" on him. Character and plot came from high culture and also from daily newspapers and the magazines of mass culture: *The Great Gatsby* expresses freely its own observations and reliance on popular songs, movies, scandal sheets, "news," and even advertisements. In the background also are other sources, some of them proceeding from Public Philosophy. There were many writings by William James that echo in this text; and also writings by others who referred themselves to him. As I've noted, in the guise of the amateur in *Flappers and Philosophers,* Fitzgerald let the reader know that he knew (or at least knew about) this part of the marketplace.

We might think of the way that recent scholarship has illuminated the effects of Darwinism on novel writing, its provision of the great themes (and some of the great metaphors) of chaos, chance, natural redundancy, and sexual selection.[12] Late nineteenth-century fiction was forced to deal with these theoretical presences, even to adjust its language into appropriate metaphor. Early twentieth-century fiction too has its bedrock, and we may expect to find in it certain refractions: the questioning of idealism; the comparison of past to present; the issue of true American identity; and the (frequent) examination of a "modern society . . . devoid of moral tension," all issues scrutinized by James and debated with great vigor over Fitzgerald's lifetime.[13]

James was a central figure in the world that Fitzgerald began in. Jacques Barzun points out that he set the terms for the examination of American intellectual and social life and was admired by intellectuals from Whitehead and Holmes to Gertrude Stein.[14] He was especially interested in the discerning power of fiction and believed "art was an extension and clarification . . . of experience."[15] Mencken recalled him as himself a public figure, the official Great Thinker of America from the century's opening until his eventual replacement by John Dewey: "The reign of James . . . was long and glorious. For three or four years running he was mentioned in every one of those American *Spectators* and *Saturday Reviews* at least once a week, and often a dozen times. . . . there was scarcely a serious rival."[16] Mencken adds (not entirely happily) that James's "ghost went marching on" for years after his death in 1910. He was being nothing less than literal: in 1922, the year of the setting of *The Great Gatsby,* the February 15 issue of the *New Republic* ran a full-page ad on the treatment of "Nerves" that quoted the *Baltimore Evening Sun* on James's accessible mind and style; the March 1 issue carried Walter Lippmann's introductory chapter of *Public Opinion,* which ended with extensive remarks on James and national culture; the April 12 issue carried John Dewey's "Pragmatic America" piece, which referred itself in both title and body to James's views on American identity; and the June issue of the *Dial* ran George Santayana's piece on Jamesian psychology. That year, when *Civilization in the United States* (a reformist survey of American culture) appeared, it contained the statement, "In even the briefest and most random enumeration of towering native sons, it is impossible to ignore the name of William James. Here for once the suffrage of town and gown, of domestic and alien judges is unanimous. . . . he is far more than a great psychologist, philosopher, or literary man."[17]

The voice of William James could be heard echoing in every argument over the shortcomings of democracy. He very nearly monopolized the subject of American social and personal identity, and as long as Lippmann and Dewey were alive, there would be continuing allusions to and development of his own arguments. The focus was on American lives: *Pragmatism,* to mention only one of his shelf of works, contains central ideas on our individual conceptions of truth; on our responsibility to live within defined space and time; on the evidence of "mere facts," which are so unsatisfactory to the "romantic" mind. The more absolute our adorations, James wrote, the more likely that we will lose "contact with the concrete parts of life."[18] James was greatly concerned with heroism and particularly with the energies that made it possible. I will allude to these points more fully when the text concentrates on Gatsby; meanwhile other issues of Public Philosophy ought to be reviewed.

Public Philosophy frames some of the questions asked by the text of this novel, and it provides an ironic background for the answers to these questions. At its heart is the idea of obligation. It states relentlessly our duties to our own individual development and toward others in the social unit. It is highly specific, and often novelistic in its practice, picturing the dilemmas of philosophy in anecdotes of social life. It is full of exemplary American characters who have to make choices. It is consciously literary: James's famous address "Is Life Worth Living?" begins with a citation from Shakespeare, moves to Walt Whitman and then to Rousseau, and from there recites, at enormous length, the poetry of James Thomson. James invokes Leopardi and Ruskin and Marcus Aurelius, and works his way through the sinuousities of Carlyle.[19] Throughout, his assumption is that literature and philosophy have common ends and tactics. In another essay, "The Moral Philosopher and the Moral Life," he argues that ethics must be allied with literature: "I mean with novels and dramas of the deeper sort."[20] This, incidentally, was a reiterated point for James, for Royce, and especially for John Dewey. As far as James, the principal figure of Public Philosophy was concerned, he specifically intended to find common ground with poetry and fiction. He invited authorship dealing with his ideas. He took pains, like Theodore Roosevelt, to address an audience of the young and educated—his best-known addresses containing among them "talks" delivered at colleges and to teachers.

The tactical subjects of Jamesian Public Philosophy are resistance to the temptations of a deeply materialistic culture, moral and intellectual improvement, the conversion of natural energies to worthy purposes, and our social duties in America. Public Philosophy provides part of the background for the debates in Fitzgerald's narrative concerning family and human relationships and for the hopeful concept of individualism.

The dialogue of the opening chapter takes up certain specific issues. Here and throughout, the Buchanans use a moral and often moralistic terminology. Even this early in the story, Tom and Daisy and Jordan invoke (or defend or passively follow) rules that mean very little to them. And when they want most to be subjective, they most invoke the canonical language of idealized American social relations. They keep telling us what they believe, which requires that we recognize not only what they are saying but what relationship they have to their statements.

One subject of discussion is the idea of American "civilization." That would seem to be a condition achieved through the slow and painful advance of mind and art—but it turns out that "civilization" in this narrative is something assumed, conferred, and denied. The idea of being truly American is an important part of Tom Buchanan's own identity. In some ways, he is no different from Gatsby: he only picks a different model. He emphasizes and exaggerates his Americanism—although the suspicions raised in the novel's opening pages about the nineteenth-century background unavoidably shade *his* argument because Tom looks ever backward to the *verities* of "the Victorian era." He will prove to be increasingly concerned with empty "decencies," which for him are the (usefully) nominal forms of respectability.

Like the word "promise," the word "civilization" was highly contextual in the early twenties. In fact, it was a word often encountered in print in the summer of 1922.[21] Tom gets his ideas from magazines and the popular press, conceivably even (Tom is, under authorial impulsion, looking slightly ahead, while Fitzgerald is looking backward from 1924–1925) from debate over an important book that I have cited, *Civilization in the United States,* edited by Harold Stearns. Tom's own literary sources have told him, in opposition to writers like Stearns who protested the distinction, that America is a product of "Nordic" or of "Anglo-Saxon" culture. They have also told him that American "civilization" is threatened by black emigration from the southern states and white immigration from eastern Europe. It is our social duty to restore the native balance. This was a respectable position at the moment, restated by the White House and Congress, validated by journals like the *Saturday Evening Post,* diffused to an active audience that includes Tom Buchanan, accepted by a more passive audience that includes Daisy and Jordan Baker. But American "civilization" and its synonyms like "culture" and "society" were ideas under stress and in the process of change.

Fitzgerald mirrors debate on American culture from the time when the novel takes place to the time when it was being written. For example, in 1924 H. L. Mencken summarized the view that the "arts" and "sciences" were now being advanced by *recent* immigrants to this country who admittedly did not come from northern or "Nordic" Europe.[22] And the defense of nativist and other forms of racist culture had begun to be excoriated (in the spring of 1922) by Walter Lippmann.[23] Such ideas, Lippmann observed, were simply ammunition for the untalented. Hannah Arendt has noted that these ideas began to be circulated in the last quarter century of that "Victorian era."[24] But of course, under the influence of the debate on immigration, they were at their most intense exactly within the period 1922–1924.

A second issue concerns internal social change, and Morton White reminds us that Public Philosophy in the "golden age" of James, Royce, Santayana, and Dewey consistently debated the transformation of America from provincial to urban life.[25] The city was a special topic— especially in its new and amoral incarnation. James wrote often about the uneasy relationship of the urban, isolated "individual" to traditional, provincial ideas of society. The city of moderns and modernism offered too much free-

dom and far too little restraint. It was morally anonymous. The sexually predatory Tom Buchanan understands that it is his new natural habitat and volunteers
that he'd be a "God Damn fool to live anywhere else" (12).
New York is necessary for Gatsby but also for Tom. A
number of pieces written by Mencken at this time (1924–
1927) depicted New York (from Baltimore's more rustic
point of view) as a paradigm for sexual opportunism.[26]

The idea of the provincial itself was an American issue, as it is in Fitzgerald's text. We are made to experience East Egg through the sensibility of the provinces.
Josiah Royce, a revisionist Jamesian, understood the conflict that lies at the heart of *The Great Gatsby* between
what Nick calls "the warm center of the world" and "the
ragged edge of the universe" (6). Royce was himself convinced that life was at its best in "the provincial community," and he added, emphatically, that only "in the province" is the "social mind . . . naturally aware of itself as at
home with its own."[27] The values of the "provincial" life
matter greatly in this text and in Fitzgerald's short stories
in the early twenties about the fascinations of the Deep
South and Midwest. The "social mind" of those places is
the subject of his work; aware of itself, as Daisy is when
she describes herself ironically as having become "sophisticated" out of her own Southern innocence. We are
reminded often of moral relativity, and also of the relativity imposed by the swift passage of time. Not Gatsby
alone but all the main characters of the novel have been

something other than what they are and have changed from their provincial identity. They are working out a dilemma of American philosophy.

Royce had even suggested the plot for an American narrative: as Morton White states Royce's position, "alienation might be overcome . . . if Americans were to combat the forces leading to detachment and loneliness by repairing to the provinces."[28] It is a plot that Fitzgerald considers; although it might be said that he changes the scenario from a cavalry charge to an exhausted retreat here and in "The Ice Palace" and in *Tender Is the Night.*

John Dewey assumed that the Jamesian philosophy centered on "the free responses of the American people to the American scene."[29] Santayana thought, however, as did Lippmann, that the responses of the public might have little freedom to display. The latter was a highly industrious meliorist, but the former eventually abandoned the world of urban, democratic realities.[30] There was simply too much competition among new peoples for old ideas to prevail. And the authority of ethics was in any case giving way before that of consumer society, with its many subjective gratifications. People got their ideas now from the *Saturday Evening Post,* not the Public Philosophy created by William James. Some of them, like Tom Buchanan, got their ideas from the best-sellers of racism. Others, like Daisy Buchanan, listened only to what the "most advanced people" thought (17), which is to say, they listened only to those editorialists whose ideas had been diffused onto the North Shore.

In *The Great Gatsby* we have been plunged into public issues since the moment of entering the text. Sequentially, do we have a true relationship to our past? What in fact are the "fundamental decencies" (5)? Are the great "secrets" of our world only about banking and credit and investment securities? Does wealth imply more than its own enjoyment? Finally, do words actually mean anything? Or do we simply spout allegiances into vanishing air? Some of these issues are directly stated, often in the interrogative mode: Daisy, characteristically, wants to know what people do with their lives; Tom insists that we live up to the moral challenge of keeping "control of things" (14). Nick wonders about the right response to the many insincerities of which a social moment is constituted. But "insincerity" fails to convey the full character of the issues. The first chapter, which is indeed about the American scene, is rich in the statement of moral conflicts and their embodiment:

> "Good night," called Miss Baker from the stairs. "I haven't heard a word."
>
> "She's a nice girl," said Tom after a moment. "They oughtn't to let her run around the country this way."
>
> "Who oughtn't to?" inquired Daisy coldly.
>
> "Her family."

"Her family is one aunt about a thousand years old. Besides, Nick's going to look after her, aren't you, Nick? She's going to spend lots of week-ends out here this summer. I think the home influence will be very good for her."

Daisy and Tom looked at each other for a moment in silence. [18–19]

The passage is illustrative of the fictions that govern the narrative. There is, first of all, a certain collusion: unwilling agreement about a socially acceptable but demonstrably false idea. Here, as later when we debate the same subjects of "home" and "family" at the Plaza, a social standard is invoked that may itself be a fiction—and bears a false relationship to the acts and ideas appealing to it.

The phrases "home" and "family" have a large presence elsewhere in the text. They are or should be fixed points of reference, but by the time Fitzgerald finishes with them they carry doubts and resentments. Jordan means the opposite of what she says; and the opposite meaning is that nothing harmful to home values has occurred. It is a wonderful exercise in manner and style, with Tom, a kind of Elbert Hubbard in place, thinking of the family as a moral agency with powers of supervision; while Daisy, more modern and acute, is quick to point out that the specific "family" he has in mind no longer exists. Jordan's aunt is later described as "senile," a phrase that may be generically representative. Tom believes that it is a bad thing for girls to run around the country alone, which may be why Daisy answers his tradition-mongering so "coldly." She understands that he means Jordan is available to men like himself. In spite of the revelations of the evening, the "family" relationship of the Buchanans remains *virgo intacta,* and "the home influence" will be very good for a woman on her own. That last phrase cited is highly compressed, stating a lie about a truism in a way that binds those who hear it to knowing consent to its reinterpretation. The putative relationship of Jordan and Nick is a fiction on Daisy's mind, probably compensatory. Daisy has the compensatory habit of mind, stating things as if they were to be done. The last line of the passage, about silence, has much to say. It is one of the conspiratorial moments shared by Tom and Daisy—and a reminder to the readers that we must do as they are doing, reflect for a moment on the tangled meanings of discourse.

Perhaps it is fitting that the first page of most editions of *The Great Gatsby* invokes the seismograph, because the text, even in its background, records the collision of tectonic plates. The word "family" is encountered not only in the Public Philosophy of the golden age but in mass cult writing of the twenties—even in advertisements it generally means the combination of race, class, and, especially, religion. It is a very Protestant word, something like the word "friends" used so often by Trol-

lope to illustrate the extension of identity into relationship. Tom and Daisy manifest a kind of benevolence important to their own self-conception by talking about
their own family and its extension into the (supposed)
marriage of Nick and Jordan. Their benevolence is a role.
There are no true imperatives for them, which suggests
something about what James called lives "devoid of moral
tensions."

The terms of the novel are (in part) givens: its beginning opposes "east" and "west" in the same sense that
Royce opposes the unalienated heartland "province" to
the amoral metropolis. He and James doubted that values
bred by close association and long sacrifice could hold up
or even be transferred to the urban realm. What of new
values and ideas? The presence in the text of Tom's argument (or daydream) about "science and art and all that"
echoes another American issue. As I've briefly noted,
"science" and "art" were being produced by immigrant
Americans, not, as Tom might wish, by "Nordics." But
more specifically, as the culture changed its visual imagery and codes, from posters and advertisements to
magazine illustrations, nativists added to their political
worries the issues of communicable "beauty" and the loss
of "tradition." There is not much moral affirmation in
cubism. Tom Buchanan invokes, echoes, and vulgarizes
many public statements on culture and American identity: in 1925, the year of publication of *The Great Gatsby*,
John Dewey kept up the debate, writing about contemporary uncertainty over those very "sciences" and "arts"

and their social meaning.[31] For Dewey, the new art was the symbol of new realities, stating visually the entry of new groups into democratic public life. The new art forces us to ask ourselves whether we have the will to re-shape understanding, *to accommodate to change.* Dewey on art is also Dewey on politics: the mind cannot rightly function without an idea of the "new" even as pertaining to the old; *all* things must be mentally renewed because all of our perceptions are relentlessly sequential. Tom understands that particular message embedded in the debate on what "art" may be and who does it.

He will later in the narrative invoke the familiar metaphor of "order." Tom Buchanan wants to sound philosophical, and he does—largely because he repeats and debases Josiah Royce's famous essay entitled "The Moral Order" in our lives.[32] In that essay Royce criticizes someone who is very like Tom Buchanan, the American moralist who is all intention and no action; Royce describes the formalistic appeal to empty words as completely "vicious" and "a deliberate forgetting of what one already knows." Tom is a type that Public Philosophy has encountered. James, a voice of American social conscience, "would become famous for his sincere call to members of the patrician class" to "understand and sympathize" with the changed conditions of American life and particularly with those less fortunate.[33] But Tom's response is to see America—and "the modern world" of which it is a part—as a pigsty. He and Daisy will "retreat" from it, close themselves off hermetically from present realities. The response itself is an American issue, transplanted by Fitzgerald from contemporary arguments on the need to come to terms with the times.

These great arguments, which throughout Fitzgerald's lifetime had been addressed by great and deeply sympathetic minds, are now echoes in a vacuum chamber. It is not only that Tom both invokes and debases them: Nick cannot preserve them. Perhaps one should say, he cannot at this point defend them. But he will learn through experience the need to act on the basis of (outmoded) moral conviction.

To recall Fitzgerald's own analysis, stated in 1921: "The younger generation has been changing all thru the last twenty years." He was an astute observer and an accurate witness: in 1904 James had written, "Life is confused and superabundant, and what the younger generation appears to crave is more of the temperament of life in its philosophy. . . . I seem to read the signs of a great unsettlement." He was referring, according to Jacques Barzun, to the way modern times would look at the permanence of truth itself.[34] James worried that the time might come when even our standards would not be understood, so that human activity would no longer be based upon consciousness and intention.

The first chapter has been an echo chamber of some truths and many fictions. Its language states a good deal of what we thought we intimately knew. But most of the untruths have applied to exactly that: the known and fa-

miliar and even sacred. Words that echo enlightened intellectual history have been drained of their sincerity. In
part, that is purely tactical: such things happen when you
get your information from magazines and best-sellers.
But there really has been a great loss: a profound and I
think majestic dialogue about the way our lives should be
lived has been echoed by those unable to comprehend it.
But the reader intuits more than the devolution of ideas:
sacred words have lost their power to identify meanings.
We hardly know what "order" is. We may be "home," as
Nick says, but we don't really know where we are.

The dishonest evening (in its entirety "a trick of some
sort" [17]) has hidden vital ideas through words that
would normally express them. Tom Buchanan gives us
the idea of a country still bound together by his own selective traditions. But both character and speech have in
this narrative become part of the "basic insincerity" perceived by Nick Carraway in our actual American "civilization." The introductory chapter ends with Nick and
Gatsby under the local heavens, where incommunicable
gesture is an ultimate form of sincerity. There is no dialogue, only what a Broadway musical has rightly called
the music of the night. Real feeling may have to find a different kind of myth and language to put the connection
between desire and action.

2

Demos

The opening chapter of *The Great Gatsby* describes the rich under the fading authority of American values. The second chapter describes another and competing social realm, with ideas that never saw the inside of a library. Some of its subjects are sexual desire, a stunning level of vulgarity, and the acquisition of a new American identity through endless goods and services. Much display is involved, and there is an implicit satirical attitude toward excess, but there is also acceptance of its mental and carnal energy. And there is something else, the recognition of how "Materialism and Idealism in American Life" are connected. The phrase is the title of a famous essay of Santayana, in which he points out that "when the senses are sharp," and the heart "warm" and the spirit "vital"—and the mind uninformed—we necessarily pursue our ideals the only way we know how, as if they had material form. American ideals are about "number," "measure," and "contrivance," which is to say they are about promises fulfilled in the present, when we want them.[1] Or to take Myrtle Wilson, who has a by no means contemptible mind, "You can't live forever, you can't live forever" (31).

There is, however, a debit side to idealist materialism. Finding Myrtle's apartment in Manhattan is something like traversing the hamlet of Fish (in "The Diamond As Big as the Ritz") toward another fantasy of self-realization. The valley of ashes is an initiatory obstacle: Nick cannot see out of it, and Myrtle will not escape it. There are two connected implications, the first of them religious. A text that dreams of Eden and of things "eternal" has in it also the end of all things. As for the beginning, it revises the opening pages of the book of Genesis in which the operational verb is "to see" and the necessary adjective is "good." Blindness is essential in reversing the advent of creation from chaos, hence the specific defect of Dr. Eckleburg, which matches the difficulty of Nick Carraway's own perception. The passages have often and rightly been traced to *The Waste Land*.[2] But there is somewhat more to the religious background, even to the reminder that Dr. Eckleburg imitates Milton's Holy Spirit also "brooding on the vast abyss." Fitzgerald intentionally diminishes the religious content, making echoes out of once firm allusions. And to connect beginnings to endings, the opening of this chapter, like its closure, with characters wandering through the smoke, is a Purgatory scene, written by a novelist recently Catholic about the unraveling of Protestant order.

Certain secular meanings follow from the religious meanings, as they had in debate from William James through Walter Lippmann. In *Pragmatism* James had argued that, in the absence of religion in the early twentieth century, two things were bound to happen, the first being "the enlargement of the material universe" and the second a consequent "diminution of man's importance." As James summed up of the world in the coming decades, "the vision is materialistic and depressing."[3] As for Doctor Eckleburg, in continuing this debate, Lippmann described the "problem of unbelief" as part of another and possibly larger problem. For Lippmann, religion dead meant materialism alive. We are now in a position, he wrote, in which men and women have "ceased to believe, without ceasing to be credulous." But this has only meant the replacement of meaningful "moral authority" by "coercion in opinions, fashions and fads."[4] In short, the substitution of the marketplace for all other sources of valuation. If the absence of religion leads directly to commercial materialism, then George Wilson may be quite right about a billboard's divinity. And Fitzgerald's connection between the "dust" and "ashes" that are the residue of material life and also the residue of Christian liturgy becomes an intelligible part of a larger debate.

The description emphasizes national meanings. The

"forms" of the valley of ashes are imitative, recapitulating the American country landscape of ridges and hills and gardens and also the "houses and chimneys and rising smoke" (21) of an industrial skyline opposed to it in more than one way. The landscape is a backdrop for human activity. Its subordination to human activity is a form of silent commentary.

This may be the American scene as visualized in a particular (and highly polemical) way. Sir Arthur Conan Doyle's "The Valley of Fear" had appeared serially in 1915 in illustrated numbers of *Strand Magazine*. Frank Wiles, Arthur Keller, and especially Frederic Dorr Steele, who worked on many of the famous Sherlock Holmes stories, contributed dark, moody drawings that followed the text. These drawings, which are faithful to Doyle, depict the American personae of "The Valley of Fear" in terms of flawed materialism, mindless agents of money and power. And the story itself views America from a detached, civilized European viewpoint that regards unhallowed wealth and crime as principal elements of American culture.

Our first sight of this particular American scene is from a railroad car traversing a horrendous and "desolate" valley of coal, smoke, and ashes (Fitzgerald's "valley of ashes" is also "desolate"). There are "great heaps of slag and dumps of cinders" looming everywhere. The crowds of men who work here are dusty, covered with black grime, anonymous. The scene impedes perception because everywhere are "clouds of drifting smoke."[5] But we can see through the smoke the tracks and the little service communities along the right-of-way for those who must work among the ashes.

Doyle, a decidedly hostile witness, connects the money (he calls it the "hidden wealth" of the New World) to be made here with a cultural and national scene that is dead, ugly, and squalid. He does have a certain admiration for American dynamism as in "A Study in Scarlet," but that is overshadowed by contempt for its material form. We are required to see the scene as his protagonist does, with "mingled repulsion and interest" (Doyle, 1463–69).

Within this "valley of fear" or American social-economic reality, the pursuit of great wealth is more than industrial. Profit is suspect and fortunes are made by crime. American wealth is connected only dimly to production and more directly to fraud. In this particular story a woman who lives among the ashes is taken away by a man who conceals his identity. He later changes it entirely, migrating from classless American to British gentry. But he is found out and eventually dies for his beliefs.[6]

In Doyle, Americans are prisoners of their own success, and the story proceeds through scenes of imprisonment and punishment and narrow escape. But there is nothing in Doyle about the greater literary theme that was on Fitzgerald's mind, the liberation of self through change. And Doyle has nothing of Fitzgerald's and America's imagination about the liberating effects of money, an idea impenetrable to gentility.

Tom is at this point in his sexual biography no longer driving off with chambermaids. Myrtle is inflicted on his friends in popular restaurants, which suggests the domesticity of their relationship. They have a daytime relationship and an entourage that imitates marriage. Tom treats Myrtle like a wife, leaving her at table while he talks to men who matter. She will act like a wife, putting together a domestic milieu in the parlor that will legitimize the bedroom. It is no wonder that she confuses all this with marriage. But it should be noted that Myrtle, of course, has her own agenda, to divorce Wilson and marry Tom. She has developed a coherent and even literary account of this agenda, suggesting that a good deal of thought has gone into its formulation. The story she communicates may not be a true story, but it is a good script.

The most recent movie version of *The Great Gatsby* (Paramount, 1974) mistakenly made Myrtle beautiful. She is not a jazz baby. Myrtle is large, bosomy, hippy, "thickish," and fleshy. She is not part of modernism, and she will not look like those female bodies featured in *Vanity Fair* in 1922. Myrtle is an exaggerated reminder of ideal female form around 1910 when Tom, one supposes, formed his own sexual ideals. Myrtle fulfills, however, at least one standard of sexual attraction: her "vitality" matters, especially in its implicit contrast to Daisy's languor.

The sexuality of *both* women is tied to class and money. In the age of servants and extended households rich men first experience sex with women like Myrtle.

Sex defers to "decencies." Tom waits for Myrtle "out of sight" and has her sit "discreetly" in another railroad car (23). Tom's domestic benevolence still drives his imagination—the reason Myrtle is going to New York is that "it does her good to get away" (23), which sounds like advice from an especially fatherly physician. Tom stays in character for some time, telling Nick, "Myrtle'll be hurt if you don't come up to the apartment" (25).

Something has happened between the moment that Myrtle boards the train to New York and her exit at Penn Station. She is sensate when we first meet her, and, even in the self-censored language of the early twenties she embodies, exudes sexuality. The train ride to New York repeats the first ride when she meets Tom Buchanan; and that story, retold to Nick, is in fact deeply sexual. It is about a woman picked up by a man who gets her "excited" in a public place by pressing against her. But when Myrtle gets off the train in New York with Nick and Tom, we don't hear much more about her wet lips and smoldering nerves.

On the other side of the river Myrtle is what she wants to be, which is haute middle-class. Her apartment brings to novelistic life Santayana's shrewd observation about the American "idealist working on matter."[7] Myrtle deals in time and quantity. Judging from her apartment, she has thought a great deal about forms for her imagination, about measure, and especially about modes or "contrivance." Myrtle is firmly located in the world of things and knows or wants to know the answer to every issue that can be materially understood. Her possessions and aspirations have particular meanings.[8]

Myrtle knows that a matron, which is what she wants to be, does not walk or drive alone—advertisements of the twenties routinely show scenes of dog and matron as a matched pair. The arrangement carries over even to cartoons. Myrtle understands that she needs to own a dog recognizable to other matrons. It should have a definite role or function, an agreed-upon social value, and the right disposition "for the apartment" (24). Having ascertained these things, she has done her duty as she understands it.

Myrtle's mind has been tactically shaped: when she reaches the apartment building on 158th Street, she gets out of the cab as if she belongs there. The first thing she does is to gather packages, the second is to assemble witnesses in order to legitimate her presence: "I'm going to have the McKees come up," she announced as we rose in the elevator. "And of course I got to call up my sister too" (25). Again the family-and-friends motif, but this time in a different key: it matters a great deal that she should be part of a society, more insistently than going to bed with

Tom. That happens, but the bedroom means less in this apartment than the living room. The living room is where the real energies of Myrtle's imagination are displayed.

This chapter has a two-way relationship with the marketing of industrial products: it introduces many products (among them are ideas and self-conceptions); and it uses the language of "advertisement" and "magazines." First, the products: Myrtle seems not to own or be interested in what jazz babies or gold diggers want. She lives in Washington Heights, not off Fifth Avenue. She buys from drugstores and vendors and department stores—there are no jewels visibly in her apartment. Her apartment is not interior-decorated but looks like a crowded showroom. In it are things that Fitzgerald emphasizes are mass produced: among them magazines and photographs that are both provided by and define the idea of mass marketing. They have given Myrtle the images with which to objectify their ideas. Nick understands the new relationship between ideas and things; between media, movies and ads, and our imaginations that derive from them. He describes McKee, asleep in a chair with his fists clenched, looking "like a photograph of a man of action" (31). The subject unconsciously conforms to a cliché of the marketplace, while our consciousness finds that it must refer itself to its language. Throughout the narrative Nick will see things in terms of already printed pictures, illustrations, "news," and "scenes." We will be reminded of books, magazines, advertisements, and movies in relation to other characters. Not only are these characters—Myrtle in particular—swamped by the goods and services of industrial democracy but they have come to understand ideas and things in terms of the marketing of those ideas and things.

Myrtle has had good reasons for letting four taxicabs drive by at Penn Station before selecting a new one, "lavender-colored with grey upholstery" (24). Her style is not arbitrary: in May 1922, *Vanity Fair* takes very seriously a certain issue of social choice and asks, "How Shall We Decorate Our Car?" Readers are told that "greys and tans" show not only "good taste" but imply monied "culture and conservatism." It is also a good thing to broaden our palette and choose "delicate colours" that "harmonize" with "personality." Myrtle takes these cues sensibly, understanding the range of culture she is expected to master—and fully aware of the kind of personality she is trying to display. Lavender suggests an ideal of moneyed tastefulness; while a gray interior goes with her communication of "impressive hauteur," signifying that she should indeed become Mrs. Buchanan.

Myrtle has a lot to say between arriving at Penn Station and getting out of the cab on 158th Street, but only three words in her dialogue are over one syllable long. The contrast is heavy: Nick talks about "a dozen very recent puppies of an indeterminate breed" but Myrtle, who has no intellectual inhibitions, asks simply, "What kind are they?" (24). Nick stands back isolated in his education, while Myrtle and the man who looks like Rockefeller have one of the great subliterary conversations in American literature.

Myrtle uses only three active verbs, and two of them are different forms of the same thing, "get" and "got," "is" and "are." In 1925 Hemingway had just been praised because he could put "a whole character into a phrase, an entire situation into a sentence." Each of his words counted "three or four ways."[9] Myrtle's vocabulary establishes intention, identity, probability, cost, and character in an even higher ratio: "I want to get one of those dogs. . . . I want to get one. . . . They're nice to have. . . . What kind are they? . . . I'd like to get one of those. . . . you got that kind? . . . I think it's cute. . . . How much is it?" (24). At the apartment, Myrtle will be even more verbally economical, shaping an entire language from two operative verbs: "I've got to get. . . . I've got to get" (31).[10] In fact, *one* of these verbs is in itself a language, meaning at the same time having, getting, and wanting, the primal things ("I got to write . . . I got to do" [31]) on Myrtle's mind. Something else about these phrases ought to be noted, though: even at this primary stage they have been delicately transformed. Under Myrtle's careful supervision they are no longer what they might have been: "I gotta getta. . . . I gotta getta." Fitzgerald has given Myrtle very short sentences at this point in the text to indicate that she is at the limits of mannerism. There are heavy pauses between statements, and Myrtle is trying hard to bridge spaces and enunciate. As she gains confidence she explores longer statements but always in a language borrowed from her sources.

Recent scholarship has pointed out the importance of spatial relationships in realist fiction. Of special interest is the "conflicted" representation of rentals and possessions:

> The realists are preoccupied with the problem of inhabiting and representing rented space, from the middle-class apartment of the Marches, to Lily Bart's boardinghouse and Hurstwood's rented beds, to the hotel rooms of Norma Hatch and Carrie. Rented spaces constitute a world filled with things neither known nor valued through well-worn contact, but cluttered instead with mass-produced furnishings.[11]

Myrtle's apartment consists of "a small living room, a small dining room, a small bedroom" (25). But it has more of the evidence of mass production than it can contain. Some of the things in it (tapestried furniture, photograph, magazines) are not only reproductions but reminders of reproduction, so that there is a sense of endless reflection. Her place is in fact "a world filled with things" and itself reproduces that metaphor. Myrtle's space is, in addition, what another critic has called a "theatre of action." That is to say, it has been "bounded and shaped" and "is no longer merely a neutral background." Clearly,

Myrtle is theatrical and knows how to deliver lines (and try on costumes and exhibit certain kinds of gesture). To that extent, she is liberated from the inconvenience of her identity. However, if spaciousness implies freedom, this apartment implies the opposite.[12]

Newspapers, magazines, and commodities show "the growing dominance of a mass culture," which is in effect a "national market."[13] The things in Myrtle's place are in more than one sense not her own. Where does she find constituted authority for them?

Advertising Age reports that there was "plenty of copy to explain" how products could change your life in the early twenties.[14] There was far more copy in ads of the twenties than there is now, hence ads were far more verbally instructive about manners and their expression. They were intentionally educational (which is to say that they informed the consumer how to become an ideal and higher social form of herself through acquisition of the right things). And they were aimed at those who had recently come into the market because of the expanding economy. Myrtle is literate enough to participate in the new marketplace of the twenties, although she does have to be brought up to speed. Fitzgerald has given her the equipment of the new classes: she works, goes to movies, is halfway emancipated from her husband, buys magazines—and has aspirations about reinventing her life. The classic *Middletown,* published at the end of the decade, recognizes the connection between an impressionable new audience with those aspirations and new marketing tactics. In judging the rate of consumption in early 1923, *Middletown* comes down hard on newspaper ads that pretend to answer "questions pertaining to your life—love, courtship, marriage, business, etc." It knows that *any* public philosophy we may have had in America has been displaced and that "the credulity of a large section of the population is exploited" by the promise that consumption is a way of developing social character.[15]

Of equal importance, *Middletown* observes that movies too are sources of identity, offering the lower middle classes the "vicarious living" of "a happy sophisticated make-believe world."[16] But there is something more complex at work, because feature films are played "synchronously" at movie houses—and are reinforced synchronously by current issues of *Live Stories, True Story, Telling Tales,* and *Motion Picture Magazine.* These magazines have by 1924–1925 captured an enormous audience of women, giving them, among other things, the plot of "sex adventure" and high living with "a moral conclusion."[17] Myrtle's scandal sheets and movie magazines give her the plot of her imagined life.[18]

We hear about Gatsby from an unlikely source, Myrtle's sister Catherine, who informs us that he is Kaiser Wilhelm's cousin. Much information enters the text through intervening levels of fiction, as we've already seen at the Buchanans. Characters accounting for their own biographies and philosophies use the techniques of literature. Gatsby is only one among many in this story who use "speech" to reformulate "God's truth." The following is an exchange of biographies, with Mrs. McKee beginning her life story:

"I almost made a mistake too," she declared vigorously. "I almost married a little kyke who'd been after me for years. I knew he was below me. Everybody kept saying to me, 'Lucille, that man's way below you!' But if I hadn't met Chester he'd of got me sure."

"Yes, but listen," said Myrtle Wilson, nodding her head up and down. "At least you didn't marry him."

"I know I didn't."

"Well, I married him," said Myrtle ambiguously. "And that's the difference between your case and mine."

"Why did you, Myrtle?" demanded Catherine. "Nobody forced you to."

Myrtle considered.

"I married him because I thought he was a gentleman," she said finally. "I thought he knew something about breeding but he wasn't fit to lick my shoe." [29–30]

We already know that Mrs. McKee is not only "handsome" but "horrible." The first attribute suggests that she can make sexual choices; the second that her character is what it is in relation to others. Both are important. Her statements add up to a coherent story, but another and opposing story can be constructed out of the same materials. It is an elegant strategy, and Fitzgerald uses it more than once in the novel.

The opposing story is more probable. It begins with a tale of true love about the man "who'd been after me for years" (29). In this novel, this scenario has an echo. That Lucille is "handsome" seems on the face of it to have been verified: she's had a lover, a husband, and now Nick as a witness. But "years" is a long time without any encouragement, and this particular biography, which from beginning to end invites alternative interpretations, should probably read that she has had a long relationship that did not turn into marriage. Possibly there was a proposal, and possibly her dignity was offended—but that phrase, "I almost married" imposes limits of interpretation. If she was so much on the verge, if he almost "got" her, then the "case" was consensual.

The idea of a "mistake" supposes social levels so remote and extensive that her lover is by definition and acclaim "way below" her. It is another echo of Daisy and Gatsby—it is their story told over—and a reminder not only of imitative fantasies but of the limits of democracy. The comedy keeps echoing, there being not that many layers of distinction below the McKees in Washington Heights.

As for "horrible," the rejected (rejecting?) lover was during the affair called something other than "little kyke." Like others in the text he has lost one name but gained another. "Little kyke" is a revenge phrase, to be used ever after (that is, in this guilt-assuaging fiction) as an assurance to herself and those imagined witnesses *who are so much on her mind.* She needs to have them see her social purgation, and we see the choric quality of assent: those around her ("Everybody kept saying" [29]) were convinced by the same reasoning with which she hopes to convince this latest audience. Again, this is something Fitzgerald does repeatedly and well. The moral order of Lucille McKee's world is visibly operative. Like Daisy, who also argues from the premise that "everybody thinks so" (17), Mrs. McKee uses a certain language. She reminds us that whatever one does is visible in a democracy and that it must be accounted for in this particular democracy. She also reminds us that Tom Buchanan is not alone in his "public" opinions.

Novels of the twenties often show guilt assuaged through appeal to public opinion. There is a moment in *Babbitt* in which some of the standard enemies of public order are addressed by a traveling collar salesman: "We ought to get together and show the black man, yes, and the yellow man, his place." This is as responsive as a liturgy: " 'And another thing we got to do,' said the man with the velour hat (whose name was Koplinsky), 'is to keep those damn foreigners out of the country.' "[19] There are few innocent words in the twenties—certainly not "home," "family"—or, especially, "we."

Catherine asks Myrtle a leading question—which is directed at the reader: why did she marry Wilson when "nobody forced you to"? (30). It is an invitation to wax literary, and Myrtle is equal to the challenge: it takes a moment or two to pull together sources of memory, in this case impassioned scripts and stories about the preservation of virtue, a notable theme of Lucille McKee's version of her own life. These narratives have a level of gentility two or three social classes above their readers. The phrase "breeding" is a dead giveaway, and more needs to be said about that. For the moment, however, the reader notes that on the downward slope from dime romance to Myrtle Wilson, kissing feet has gotten mixed up with licking shoes.

Myrtle has been reading more than "Town Tattle." George Wilson stopped being a gentleman when he had to borrow a suit. Myrtle knows a good deal about social meanings: Tom, with "a dress suit and patent leather shoes" (31) conforms to newsstand gentility. But what really is a gentleman? In May 1922 *Vanity Fair* tells its upwardly aspiring audience that there is a tremendous distinction between the lower-class salesman without "good taste" or "knowledge" who imitates a false idea of gentility and the upscale customer, who should buy suits imitating those of *real* gentlemen. Some things are inbred and not acquired. Real gentlemen, in their turn, imitate real figures like the (illustrated) Earl of Worcester, who "is considered to be very well dressed," and Lord Burghersh, who is always "very smartly turned out." That is to say, these individuals are the realest gentlemen. The phrase "gentleman" means observing standards of conduct, but it also means what Myrtle and many other amateur anthropologists call "breeding"—that is to say, boots and saddles, English style, Protestant standing, social visibility, and, one hopes, inherited funds. The theme constantly and consciously plays against that of classless democracy. Here is Fitzgerald's later analysis of clothes that make the ruling class:

> With Americans ordering suits by the gross in London, the Bond Street tailors perforce agreed to moderate their cut to the American long-waisted figure and loose-fitting taste, something subtle passed to America, the style of man. During the Renaissance, Francis the First looked to Florence to trim his leg. Seventeenth-century England aped the court of France, and fifty years ago the German Guards officer bought his civilian clothes in London. Gentlemen's clothes—symbol of "the power that man must hold and that passes from race to race." [20]

But Fitzgerald means more than acquisition. When Lucille McKee and Myrtle Wilson talk about love and gentility, they are trying to impose some sort of order on their lives, even if they have to invent not only the lives but the idea of order they apply. Order in one of its forms is style. One of the reasons that Gatsby is fascinated by the idea of many changes of clothes in Daisy's household is that he, like Myrtle and Lucille McKee, has gotten his ideas about gentility from ads and magazines that suggest the completion of life through imitation—which now has its own marketplace for selves. That is why Myrtle and Lucille McKee can so unselfconsciously state their preferences for choosing new selves and argue for acceptance. They expect to be ladies as Gatsby expects to be a gentleman, and they prepare us for him. When he shows Daisy his collection of shirts, the moment is heraldic.

Fitzgerald's closure describes social geography in more than one way. It continues the idea of ascribed relationship. Out of certainties, confusion: "People disappeared, reappeared, made plans to go somewhere, and then lost each other, searched for each other, found each other a few feet away" (31). It is at the same time real, metaphorical, and metaphysical:

> Then there were bloody towels upon the bathroom floor and women's voices scolding, and high over the confusion a long, broken wail of pain. Mr. McKee awoke from his doze and started in a daze toward the door. When he had gone half way he turned around and stared at the scene—his wife and Catherine scolding and consoling as they stumbled here and there among the crowded furniture with articles of aid, and the despairing figure on the couch bleeding

> fluently and trying to spread a copy of "Town Tattle"
> over the tapestry scenes of Versailles. [32]

This is a larger and more representative moment in writing than may appear. Fitzgerald's language of dissolution and confusion has a number of analogues. His subject, when addressed by other writers, is described in terms of the ungoverned motion of physical particles or of distorting mirrors. That subject, democratic American society in the twenties, is covered by a certain topos of fiction and political philosophy. Edith Wharton's own closure to *The Age of Innocence* (1920) has one summation: "of what account was anybody's past, in the huge kaleidoscope where all the social atoms spun around on the same plane?"[21] Both Yeats and Eliot borrow from the language of spun atoms and centrifugal force and mindless motion to describe the cultural moment and its ever-shifting beliefs. Walter Lippmann writes in *Public Opinion* (1922) of "helter-skelter" civilization and "aimless" automatism and minds caught up in "a kind of tarantella" by information that they cannot understand.[22] John Dewey writes (1925) of the overwhelming problem of accounting for "phenomenal flux" in our social world while wishing for "unprecarious reality."[23]

Walter Lippmann's *A Preface to Morals* (1929) begins with the essay "Whirl Is King." There are, Lippmann writes, too many "unseen events and strange people and queer doings" for the mind to register. Facts "are detached from their backgrounds, their causes and their consequences." Experiences have "no beginning, no middle, and no end." He has an appropriate description of Nick Carraway's situation: "Such experience as comes to him from the outside is a dissonance composed of a thousand noises. And amidst these noises he has for inner guidance only a conscience which consists, as he half suspects, of the confused echoes of earlier tunes."[24] Lippmann is writing of the tone of modern experience, specifically as derived from "the machinery of intelligence" like news publication. His subject is American democracy in the twenties, an idea that has no manageable form, perhaps no correlative. Lippmann keeps to the language of cognitive disorientation so important to Eliot, to Public Philosophy, and to Fitzgerald, who has borrowed the topos of disintegrated relationship. It plays against the linearity of the narrative and especially against the powerful theme of purposeful navigation. It is a metonym for democracy, a form of life without control.

Jacques Barzun's elegant tribute *A Stroll with William James* adds example and explanation. Barzun points out that when Frazer, in his own act of closure to *The Golden Bough,* invokes an "ever-shifting phantasmagoria of thought," he means to convey the hopeless difficulty of understanding our cultural moment. The first part of our century, Barzun reminds us, gave to the rest of it the "reconstruction of the western mind."[25] Particularly as reconstruction applied to social ideas, the effect was too

troubling and confusing to order. How can life be con-
ducted in a moment when standards have disappeared
and when values from all conceivable kinds of sources
compete for our momentary attention? How can we deal
not only with social problems but with selves that change
as it were before our eyes?

Fitzgerald has exaggerated his differences with realism in order to suggest something discerned by philosophy—even the proverbial smoke-filled room is less im-
permeable than this one. This situation is more like
Plato's Cave. All of the elements of location—time, place,
distance, vision, sound—have themselves "disappeared."
Turning to stare "at the scene," (32) we see with Chester
McKee a Miltonic scene of high "confusion." One important observation is unconsciously made by the drunken
viewer: object and person have become indistinguishable. Like Hogarth's "Satire on False Perspective," everything is in the picture, but nothing makes sense relative
to anything else.[26] And indeed Fitzgerald's closure is a
"scene" (his phrase) of wrecked perspective and relationship.

Nick is within a particular situation, but he is also
within a much larger milieu. He is drunk because people
in the early twenties drink a lot—but he is disoriented,
because what he sees makes little sense. What he sees is
not the distortion of an amusement park; it is only manners, styles, and ethics made concrete. The hopeful distinction of the novel's first page, between the "normal"

and the "abnormal," will evidently not apply. It is no wonder that authors of the early twenties invoke the movement of unconscious particles, or of unpredictability, or of
the kaleidoscope for social "reality." Those are the things
that Nick sees at Myrtle's party, in which character and
identity are mutable.

3

Community and Crowd

Fitzgerald stays close to the ideas of measure, number, and contrivance that also strike Santayana in theorizing about the imagination of Americans.[1] Gatsby's establishment contains one Rolls Royce, two motorboats, five crates of oranges and lemons, eight toiling servants, and several hundred feet of catered canvas. Recognizing something, the narrator is also caught up in number and sequence, placing the divers he sees at "high tide in the afternoon," cars working between nine in the morning and "long past midnight," servants working every Monday, crates arriving every Friday, the garden disguised "once a fortnight," the orchestra not some "thin five piece affair" but big enough to fill a symphony hall (33). In half a sentence one button is pressed two hundred times in thirty minutes, giving us a sense of accomplishment that Americans recognize in life and in the act of writing. At a later moment Gatsby will say of his place, "It took me just three years to earn the money that bought it." As he says that, his eye is counting "every arched door and square tower" (71). Nick understands the logic of what he sees and he describes things—either willingly or necessarily—as Gatsby expects them to be seen.

The prose follows the patterning of ideas. It is not so much describing what happens as giving us a sense of what we should notice. Nick has filtered out all other permutations of ideas and has seen what there is to be seen not only through Gatsby's eyes but through the eyes of the representative American reader. In this way we are expected to register effects, as if we were reading realty ads. The text is full of specified numbers.

Quantifying gives a sense of regularity, and it suggests that an orderly life sequence is in process. It is one of the nervous American ways in which Gatsby, Myrtle, and even Nick assure themselves that they are going somewhere. Daisy keeps track of the passing days, Jordan of the seasons, and Nick of the years. But this metaphysic keeps reminding us of the way that information is stated in the news. That is to say, numerical precision acts as if it were moral precision, which it cannot hope to be. It will conjure up its own opposites in a panorama of indeterminacy.

Fitzgerald's third chapter develops the most extended figures of the text, suggesting order and disorder through pattern and dissonance. The dance, for example, will become a microcosm of social meanings. It will suggest the movement and the displacement of class, and it will silently state the chaos that is the other side of freedom. The chapter will raise many current issues: for example, the attractions of irrational pleasure and the moral anxieties that automatically come into play when a new sense of individualism becomes a new sense of community. It is almost as if a text were directed at the most conflictual issues in the background dialogue of sermons, political speeches, and social ethics. In the background is the thundering of philosophy and not from the school of William James alone. Theodore Roosevelt and Woodrow Wilson had been the voices of moral reasoning for anyone who matured at the time this novel takes place. They enunciated the social standards that Gatsby's society gives up.[2] As for the philosophers, Santayana wrote that our democracy should in fact allow "great diversity" but without destructive subjectivity. To be part of a "complex society" was recognizably the right expectation—but not of a society that was without "significant thoughts" and forms and experiences.[3] Literary criticism has largely agreed, finding in the third chapter of *The Great Gatsby* materialism run wild. For what I hope are good reasons, I will disagree with this view. Fitzgerald takes from the cultural context ideas that retain some usefulness, but he is forthright in his rejection of old distinctions that seem in any case to have lost their conviction.

The book's first three chapters have followed a sequence, proceeding from family relationships, to relationships that imitate them, to the absence of intelligible relationship. Certain things in this chapter are important because of their absence. Prominent among them is the idea of "community," to which I will return.

One of the things implied in this chapter is freedom from stability, something that no one who thinks takes lightly. Public Philosophy was no different from classical philosophy in its aversion to change. Tradition, historical and religious, was the ground for the exertion of its fulcrum. But Fitzgerald differs from this idea. He loves the passing moment, and he draws a line of philosophical allegiance to it. He concentrates on the attractions of the untraditional and unstable.

There was music throughout the summer nights, and it is well worth hearing—but it can be only recalled, not replayed. Men and women are "like moths," which revives one of the oldest literary statements of impermanence and the beauty of impermanence. "Whisperings" have no duration, being gone as soon as uttered. The verb forms Fitzgerald applies to his text—"spilled," "tipped out," "dissolve and form," "become for a sharp, joyous moment," "trembling," "moving"—are statements of chronology on the way to becoming their own past participles (33–34). The language is as "momentary" as that of the opening of *A Midsummer Night's Dream,* and it has some of the same values.

From this beginning we sense that there is an end, quickly reached, to all quick, bright things. The text is its own system of evidences, telling us that things happen "suddenly" and in "a burst" of expressiveness; that a "sea-change" of appearance corresponds to "the constantly changing light" (34). Less than two pages into the third chapter of *The Great Gatsby* we have been forced to think in terms of movement, change, and expiration—and of the inherent, compelling attraction of these things.

One consequence is that the story develops as much from its language as from its mythos. An entire vocabulary of evanescence is developed. It ranges from the description of arrested motion, to that of the end of a love affair, of a certain summer, and, eventually, of "the year 1922 . . . , the peak of the younger generation."[4] There are arguments about the meaning of this language of evanescence, one of them that a Platonic idea has been replaced by a Heraclitean idea, fixed values and laws by a "multiverse of process."[5] But this argument, heavily moral, tends to identify change, motion, and particularity in the text with chaos, whereas Fitzgerald seems simply to have a strong and romantic sense of phenomenology. The argument trivializes not only Gatsby's world of acquired things but Nick's response to them.

When extended, the argument states that there is not in fact much to admire about either the hero of this story or the things and people surrounding him. Fitzgerald, evidently, is about the business of making an entertaining illusion, endowing sordid material life with temporary novelistic value. We become interested not in the meretricious world of the twenties (which is incapable of real interest) but only in the novelist's description of it. I don't think that the following statement by a good critic is at all true: "The mean, phenomenal world of flesh, blood and things is of interest only to the extent that it can be transformed into 'enchanted objects.' "[6] But what if Fitzgerald intends neither to transubstantiate nor to satirize? What if he admires the phenomenal world and its moment and does not find either at all "mean" or embarrassing?

Nor do I think it true that "the background characters are defined by an essential carelessness, a moral and spiritual indifference. When they congregate, they become a faceless crowd drawn together by chance, with no purpose beyond the diversions of the moment."[7] They are not, as they have been described, pursuing "immediate gratification," are by no means "inert," and are very far from "personifications of that dissipation of human energy that attends spiritual and moral death."[8] That does sound like a sermon. But Fitzgerald's language prevents such conclusions. Entry into the third chapter of *The Great Gatsby* enforces our sense of the values of impermanence.

The dance is a powerful and complex figure with its own literary history. A recent biography of Jane Austen, who gave much thought to the meaning of dance, confirms her interest in its representation of "a larger social community."[9] The dance, although completely ephemeral, shows its institutional "relationship" to that society—and is a "display of personality—and a key to it."[10] She is acutely aware of the meanings of space and gesture as well as those of speech. She is particularly alive to the connection of dance to female sexuality. In *Pride and Prejudice,* women understand the many ways in which dance is expressive of both personal and communal meanings. Fitzgerald also takes the dance seriously and repeatedly invokes its new characteristic meanings— even when they may not be fully visible to his characters. In "May Day" Edith Bradin understands her own sexual identity in its public form: "Her bare arms and shoulders were powdered to a creamy white. She knew they looked very soft and would gleam like milk against the black backs that were to silhouette them tonight."[11] This is not entirely solipsism; the dance floor is her space but also her marketplace. Like much in that story and in *The Great Gatsby,* she is on display and for sale. In "Bernice Bobs Her Hair," the dance takes place in a self-defining space of another kind, a "combination clubroom and ballroom" before a "gallery" of witnesses.[12] It is, as in Jane Austen, the entry to the upper middle class. And it is not at all easy to get from the floor into that class. In another story, the Jelly-bean translates the class meaning of the dance instantly: "He saw the girls emerge one by one from the dressing-room, stretching and pluming themselves like bright birds, smiling over their powdered shoulders at the chaperones, casting a quick glance around to take in the room and, simultaneously, the room's reaction to their entrance."[13] But they go to other men, who can afford them. It is all a "spectacle" of the marketplace, which excludes the ineligible. At Gatsby's first party the dance is both a spectacle and a reminder to the reader of a certain kind of social change.

In *The Great Gatsby,* marriage and family are absent by default. An artificial "community" is quite literally being shaped: "The groups change more swiftly, swell with new arrivals, dissolve and form in the same breath" (34). It is a sentence that could have appeared in a particularly well written social history. A certain kind of form is being imposed and also escaped: "already there are wanderers, confident girls who weave here and there among the stouter and more stable, become for a sharp, joyous moment the center of a group and then excited with triumph glide on through the sea-change of faces and voices and color under the constantly changing light" (34). Fitzgerald's description is asexual, although we know from "May Day" what he can do with implications. Here the language is about the creation of social form in the absence of anything remotely defining it. These "background" figures have been endowed, the text specifies, not only with courage and grace and some beauty, but with daring, cheerfulness, confidence, and joy. At other points in their lives within this narrative, the background figures will be much as they appear in the catalog of guests who went, chaotically, to Gatsby's parties; at this point they reveal more than the sum of their individual characters.

The prose describes bodies in motion but also the structuring of a random moment. The crowd exists as it had been perceived by modern painting and photography: whatever the moral meanings, it is aesthetically interesting, perceptually compelling. To look through Impressionism and the movements that closely followed it is to understand that the swirls of color and the traces of energy in the mass are vital to design and are a special subject in their own right. H. L. Mencken, who had a moral quarrel with New York, nevertheless understood its aesthetic and symbolic functions. Like Edmund Wilson, he tried to define in his own prose the appearance, effect, and importance of New York's mass energies. He hated New York's Gadarene eating, drinking, and sex but concluded that, as a writer, he could well "hymn the town without loving it." About fiction on this subject, Mencken stated, "What I contend is that this spectacle [the pleasures of the crowd], lush and barbaric in its every detail, offers the material for a great imaginative literature."[14] In particular, he called attention to New York's chaotic and devolutionary "social organization;" a subject, he added, "that ought to be far more attractive to novelists than it is."[15] The crowded party scenes in this novel do the work posited by Mencken and (also throughout the 1920s) by Edmund Wilson.[16] Both understood that the pleasure-seeking crowd was a new kind of subject, often invoked as a symbol of "modern" America, and especially of rudderless democracy.

Mencken was not, I think, a good critic of *The Great Gatsby*, but he clearly understood its themes: accepting that New York was "the place where all the aspirations of the Western world meet to form one vast master aspiration";[17] and that the form this took was essentially sexual.

The night at West Egg begins in music. Imposed on the narration is the phrasing of rhythm and melody: men and women mix in an "opera of voices" and a girl "dances out alone" like Frisco (34). Sound and movement are soft and rhythmic. Throughout the text Fitzgerald uses words that echo or become musical statement: in the garden we see movement as dance and sound as "echolalia." There is, however, neither script nor choreography.

We don't hear what we expect to hear: Daisy may do a "clog" later on, but no one is doing a Charleston. The music is lyrical, part of it by "singing quartets" (41). There are horns, and a girl singing the blues, but the music of this part of the Jazz Age is orchestrated, adapted to white styles, and made for dancing. A jazz critic observes that the Carnegie Hall concert mentioned in this chapter recalls the "symphonic jazz" concert of Paul Whiteman at Aeolian Hall in 1924:

Fitzgerald did not finish the *Gatsby* manuscript until several months after the Whiteman concert, but we can be fairly certain that he is referring to Whiteman's band or to a band like his: the orchestra is described as "a whole pitful of oboes and trombones and saxophones and viols and cornets and piccolos, and low and high drums" . . . a nearly exact description of the instrumentation of the Whiteman band and of many of the leading white dance-band imitations of Whiteman. The fact that the band is "no thin five-piece affair" indicates that Gatsby is not only wealthy enough to hire such a big band to come to his house but pretentious and status-conscious enough not to have a "hot" Dixieland-style jazz band play for guests.[18]

The party involves "bourgeois acceptance" of a style that cannot be adopted as it stands.[19] But the standard will itself change, becoming, if anything, more "uncontrolled" than the style. Gatsby's party emphasizes musical order and the assimilation of "hot" style into social order. It begins with melody and rhythm—which become dissonance. It reflects the disintegration of other kinds of order, among them what in social terms is called form.

In order for Nick to get to Gatsby's first party, a long chain of events has had to take place, culminating in the appearance of a liveried chauffeur with a "surprisingly formal" (34–35) note of invitation. Nick joins Jordan's group, which "had preserved a dignified homogeneity"

(37). That last phrase is understood to have social and even political echoes. There are two suppers scheduled, which is quite a nice touch, a mark of consideration. And Gatsby has been very much comme il faut, taking care to send an enormously expensive dress to "Lucille" who has torn one on a chair. He knows about manner and magnificence—but her friend is sure only that he is buying her off. It is a microcosm of the "credulity" and "speculation" that prevent understanding of motive and act. Gatsby, who is "correct" and speaks with "formality," is trying to do something that Myrtle Wilson is also trying to do, namely to enact a social role by now a decade out of date.

The problem for both Gatsby and Myrtle—at least the problem that Fitzgerald has articulated—is that their parties break up into a kind of chaos. This disintegration may seem philosophically unimportant, but it is the subject of the text. We don't hear in the previous chapter that Myrtle's ideas are objectively wrong, foolish or impossible; we hear only that her party follows an inevitable sequence from high formality to opéra bouffe. Gatsby's parties begin with high formality but change into their opposite.

Gatsby does not understand that manner, magnificence, and form are out of style, are no longer even imaginable. Belonging to the prewar past, they are just as dated as romantic love. They have been replaced with another style, that of plutocracy. Plutocratic style is also excessive but in a very different way. It also uses huge buildings and enormous displays of wealth but not in the service of Victorian order and rectitude: it exemplifies "success."[20] Gatsby is caught between the two styles, neither of which is authentic. Part of his absurdity is the general absurdity of the alternation of social character between them. The dance provides a number of meanings: "There was dancing now on the canvas in the garden, old men pushing young girls backward in eternal graceless circles, superior couples holding each other tortuously, fashionably and keeping in the corners" (38–39). The old men and young girls have an understanding; it is inscribed in those circles. Six words—"old men pushing young girls backward"—compress the idea of financial-sexual arrangement about as far as it will go. That too is "form." But "eternal" is too long a time for anyone or any society to keep a bargain, especially a sexual one. And in a novel full of expressive motion, this scene is intentionally sterile. Those "old men" are necessarily the last visible part of "the Victorian era," and they suggest its own encoded forms. It might be said of those "superior" others so much on their dignity that the social space they occupy is far too small. The dance is at this point no longer a metaphor.

The counterpoint to the *totentanz* of high society is "a great number of single girls dancing individualistically or relieving the orchestra for a moment of the burden of the banjo or the traps" (39). We hear now of jazz and hilarity and of laughter that although vacuous is "happy" and even "uncontrollable." Nick does not indicate disapproval but admits that "I was enjoying myself now" (39). The categories of "old" and "superior" give way to a more rhythmic and interesting subjectivity. It may be under the grace of two finger bowls of champagne, but Nick comes to find the replacing scene of fluid individualism "significant, elemental and profound" (39). It is a reminder to the reader to balance his own vision: Victorian form cannot prevail—but neither can anything else. There is that movement at Gatsby's party from "happy" to "uncontrollable." The passage from one block of prose to another is the passage from one decade to another.

The evening at Gatsby's first party balances opposites: old men and young women, the married and the "single," formality against "rules of behavior associated with amusement parks" (34), the "superior" and their plebeian opposites, and always the constraints of social expectation against expressive individuality. Simply to do what the dancers are doing is to challenge the old order of things: Page Smith's social history states of this period that in the provinces in which everything originates (in this case Cleveland, Ohio), "public dance halls were governed by a municipal injunction that read in part: 'Dancers are not permitted to take either exceptionally long or short steps. . . . Don't dance from the waist up; dance from the waist down.' "[21] In the most literal sense, "form" moves visibly between metaphor and act. Fitzgerald uses a word, "rowdy" (39), that is in itself a prohibition.[22] It is the kind of behavior forbidden in Cleveland and everywhere else in provincial America under the rule of known association.

Gatsby's first party is attended by those with no mutual past, which, although a fairly standard experience after the twenties, constitutes a special kind of statement in its time. There are clearly reminders of the past in allusions to manners and styles and forms (and, of course, to all those old books with appropriately uncut pages that become visible in an interlude). But there are few imperatives left over from the past. These people are not guided by family or by other kinds of known association. In fact, the idea of association constitutes an extended joke as women repeatedly fight with their husbands or with men said to be their husbands. In these cases, form is reminiscent of vaudeville. Both men and women behave completely subjectively. There does, however, seem to be a close and clear relationship between feeling and expressiveness—at the expense of form:

> The large room was full of people. One of the girls in yellow was playing the piano and beside her stood a tall red haired young lady from a famous chorus, engaged in song. She had drunk a quantity of champagne and during the course of her song she had decided ineptly that everything was very very sad—she was not only singing, she was weeping too. Whenever there was a pause in the song she filled it up with gasping

broken sobs and then took up the lyric again in a qua-
vering soprano. The tears coursed down her cheeks—
not freely, however, for when they came into contact
with her heavily beaded eyelashes they assumed an
inky color, and pursued the rest of their way in slow
black rivulets. [42]

The breakdown of form is the expression of truth. There
are two versions of form implied: we see not only manner
but the tacit idea that the Blues—usually sung by people
who are not at all sad—themselves interpose a barrier to
feeling. Real sadness demands real tears, for which lyrics
are inadequate. Fitzgerald has already put the matter
with great force, telling us that these people come here
with "simplicity of heart" (34). They are an audience to
whom the idea of form is irrelevant. And in this respect
they constitute the great opposite to Nick's experience.

Hemingway uses the extended metaphor of dance in
The Sun Also Rises in a way that expresses revulsion from
fringe modernism and reminds us how much of Oak Park
he took to Paris. But he is very much on the same track
as Fitzgerald when he describes the dance in Pamplona.
Both are willing to give up past allegiances and to explore
a present scene with no relationship to the past but with
an indissoluble connection to a new sense of self.

At Gatsby's, the people that Nick sees are the opposite of a "community"; as the text indicates, they are a
"crowd." This seems now less antithetical than it did in

the twenties. By invoking numbers of individuals discon-
nected from the past and from each other, Fitzgerald is
reminding his readers of ongoing debates. There was a
conscious effort to make the unintelligible mass into a
definably American "community" or "society" or "public."
James, Royce, Santayana, and Lippmann each invoked
these terms, and each argued the unacceptability of that
which could not be defined in time as well as space. It is
important to be aware that the national dialogue about
true Americanism rested on this basis.

John Dewey was possibly the clearest and most organized on the subject of individuals, groups, and true
communities. In 1926 he gave a lecture entitled "Search
for the Public," describing the quest by philosophers for
more than a generation to make sense of American social
life. According to Dewey, "Association in the sense of
connection and combination is a 'law' of everything
known to exist." But, he added, "human communities"
must have traits "different from those which mark assem-
blies of electrons." What for us is simply an idea of "association" is for Dewey immutable, and he is infinitely
troubled by the idea that subjectivity should ever dominate thought or habit or self-conception.[23] James had argued in even more forceful terms that the ancestral past
"is now a part of the very structure of our mind." We exist
only in relationship to "our ancestors" whose imposed order made it possible for us to "steer our lives by rule."[24]
The community is a living reminder of history and a liv-

ing condition of citizenship. Royce was, if anything, more conservative, more traditional, and more biased in favor of "community." The social unit was rooted in time, the present being the latest form of the past. It is of some interest that Royce opposed a true "community" to what he identified as the "crowd"—and opined that a crowd might in essential points be identical with a "mob." Royce stipulated that the likely causes of cultural dissolution were the pleasures of mass materialism. Most philosophers of reform agreed that a good national life could be made up only "through individuals as members of communities."[25] Even Mencken, deeply secular and amused by pieties, wrote about mass society in terms of actual, inchoate masses besieging restaurants, revues—and then revivals.

In the face of the cultural context, Fitzgerald seems to have been more conscious and more stubborn in his identifications than we have judged. His is not the lonely crowd or the alienated crowd or the un-American crowd. He admires subjectivity greatly, and words like "strange" and "new" and "individualistically" are for him honorific. Other words, like "staid" and "superior" and "homogeneity" are self-consciously arrayed against the moral-aesthetic attractions of "spectroscopic gayety" (37). The word "old" is not honorific, and Meyer Wolfsheim certainly knows it: to "belong to another generation" is precisely *not* to be listened to. When Fitzgerald analyzed the first years of the decade, he invoked Woodrow Wilson as a symbol of the last agonies of "the Victorian era": "the old

American groaned in his sleep as he waited to be poisoned by his wife, upon the advice of the female Rasputin who then made the ultimate decision in our national affairs."[26] It is more ferocious than we expect from a nonpolitical man. It has within it the reserves of an idea that chaos is better than senility.

If his dance is an extended metaphor, then it begins with the imposition of form, is judged against the standards of social character and manner, displays a new sense of self—and devolves into inherently uncontrollable behavior not simply because sex and booze make us that way but because old standards can't prevent that anyhow. In any case, the old dispensation has made its own compromises, as we have already seen on 158th Street near Broadway. As a historian puts it, "all ethical systems are based on custom and imagination,"[27] and the one under which Americans are now operating has lost the allegiance of both. Every now and then Nick may invoke the shade of William James, but he can sound like Rousseau.

There may be closer candidates for comparison: in 1923 Havelock Ellis had published his study of an extended metaphor, *The Dance of Life,* which in part developed itself from Nietzsche. The dance was Nietzsche's own figure for the development of freedom, and in the hands of Ellis it became a long meditation on the principled opposition of individuals to "rigid formulas." Moral responsibility, Ellis wrote, does not develop from obeying rules: "Life must always be a great adventure, with risks

on every hand; a clear-sighted eye, a many-sided sympathy, a fine daring, an endless patience."[28] The old style of
moral philosophy was apt to treat life as a struggle, battle,
or test of endurance, but Ellis reinterprets it as an activity
connected with the Freudian understanding of "pleasure." Ellis, in this particular book, tried to bring to his
audience something they were already willing to believe.
But Fitzgerald recognizes the pull between values. Individualism is the end of existence, but it does not offer a
complete existence. Nor does it go unchallenged.

Fitzgerald later invoked the social-historical use of
the figure of dance when he reflected on the meaning of
the twenties: "The generation which had been adolescent
during the confusion of the War, brusquely shouldered
my contemporaries out of the way and danced into the
limelight."[29] We can see why, at Gatsby's first party, there
is so little space left for those who are guilty of the past.
The rhetorical figure is the same, but its extrapolation
differs from Yeats's "Nineteen Hundred and Nineteen,"
in which we read that "all men are dancers" or protagonists of historical rhythms.[30] In Fitzgerald, participation
in the dance is intentional and conscious.

The dance suggests a new relationship not only to
others but also to one's self. It becomes associated with
self-chosen identity. Fitzgerald did not originate the idea
of the conscious choice of identity—in one form it was already an American issue in advertising. In a considerably
loftier form it was debated by the Public Philosophy.

Here is a lucid commentary on Royce and the dangerous freedom of individualism: "Royce did not view the self as a given *substance* which is a present and finished datum to be captured in the spotlight of the inward gaze. The self is what Royce called an 'interpretation,' that is, a center of meaning. . . . The main point is that every individual has some part in determining how much of the past will enter into the ideal meaning of his life."[31] Royce also recognized that it would be a conscious choice as to "what I shall set aside as having no part in my being." Given Fitzgerald's frequent allusions to this idea, it was an issue for himself, for the "background" figures and lesser protagonists of the novel, and for Gatsby.

◢4◣

Mixed Democracy

$$B$$ridging the end of the third chapter and the beginning of the fourth is the list of guests at Gatsby's, which takes its place with a very few other Homeric catalogs. The Chromes and Willie Voltaires and the O. R. P. Schraeders rub shoulders with the Stonewall Jackson Abrams and the supremely drunk Ripley Snell. Theatrical people and politicians and the newly rich are there with women descended from the aristocracy of great American capitalists. What they have of biographies seems to be organized around sex, money, and many troubles with both, making Myrtle Wilson's little party seem as if it were done by Emily Post. The lives are disorderly but not the meanings:

Animal, vegetable, and mineral, fish and flesh, the guests, in their names, take in the world. . . . If some of the guests have been mocked by their animal names or their resemblance to animals (implying their lack of fully human dimension), the names of others involve a diminishment of stature through association with greater, more strongly directed, or heroic, lives of the past. . . . A lack of stature in the guests has also been evoked in their personal histories, their pasts or futures, which seem to be out of control, or to be subject to violent dislocations. . . . they seem scrambled together incongruously. . . . this guest list is nothing if not a satire of democracy—of a preposterous mingling, and with it a blurring and loss of identity.[1]

Most will disappear from the text, although Doctor Webster Civet and Klipspringer will continue in bit parts. But all constitute a kind of group memory of America and are signposts of events to come. In some respects the characters are interchangeable, but in one important respect they all observe rules of identity: they are organized by "clan" and family, are all somebody's "girls" or "fiancée" or "son" or "brother" or husband or "wife" (49–50). And yet the distinctions imposed by these categories are poised against the idea that some of them are "never quite the same ones in physical person but . . . so identical one with another that it inevitably seemed they had been there before" (50). The sense of ultimate change of identity is connected not only to first names that have been forgotten but to much more important "last names" that melt into their social opposites.

In order for some of those in the catalog to rise, others whose last names indicate Social Register identities have had to fall and meet them. Rise and fall and interchange were evidently on Fitzgerald's mind between 1920 and 1925: Matthew J. Bruccoli points out in his introduction to "The Diamond As Big as the Ritz" that this story had a good deal of trouble getting published because editors "found it baffling, blasphemous, or objectionably satiric about wealth."[2] The most objectionable satire was, I think, directed not at wealth's excess but at its relationship to those without it. The idea of rising to the top is in this cautionary tale more than a figure of speech. Braddock Washington offers to build a social world for his prisoners and to locate it precisely where it should be: "I've offered to have your wives, sweethearts, children, and mothers kidnapped and brought out here. I'll enlarge your place down there and feed and clothe you the rest of your lives." The prisoners object and try to reach him but slide "back to the bottom" of their glass-lined Wellsian hole in the earth. The lower-class Irish and Jews are kept there, *là-bas,* below. Rarely has the constraint on upward social mobility been so explicit. The prisoners in their dialects are definitively from "N'Yawk," a place that is in itself a contested figure of speech. And they would love to teach Washington's daughters "a lot of things" they don't know.[3] The time for that has arrived in the middle of the catalog of *The Great Gatsby*.

The criticism that I have cited above locates the catalog's central meaning in democracy—but "democracy" in 1922 was not the subject of the same argument as it is now. We have already seen the presence in the text of other words like "breeding" and "family" and "superior" and "tradition" that qualify it. Fitzgerald understands that the real issue in the early twenties is not equality but the way that people think of themselves because of the way that other people think of them. Gatsby never appeals to canons of equality, never gives readers the thrill of constituent politics. He appeals, in fact, to acknowledged social limits expressed everywhere from weekly magazines to social philosophies. The ideal, to which he subscribes, is a gentrified British rather than a prairie American style. His provincial Americanism is a dead issue. The styles on his mind, and on Myrtle's mind (and, from time to time, on Fitzgerald's mind), are those of inequality communicated by print and image: Myrtle expects to see a "gentleman" in full fig, therefore recognizes Tom when he appears on her horizon; Tom enacts patrician despair over *tempora* and mores; Gatsby may not have read Mencken yet strives to transcend plutocracy by displaying the behavior and mannerisms of a magnate. All understand that distinction matters far more than equality, gentility far more than the authenticity of mass conduct.

Fitzgerald is sympathetic to the energies of the new majority, but he is also aware that the democratic crowd in the early twenties was a literary and political trope of disorder. The writings of Public Philosophy address the crowd as a danger to community. The crowd is the reason why national character must be leavened by aristocracy: that is, by those who really *are* what Tom Buchanan wants to be. The undifferentiated "mass of men" is the opposite of what John Dewey in 1926 called "The Great Community."[4] Henry James had earlier described the foreign masses of the Jewish lower East Side as "the New York phantasmagoria."[5] The terminology, derived from optical distortion, commonly meant the physical, scientific basis for impressions. The problem was not in the viewer's consciousness but in the nature of his object. "New York" is the special case for the agonies of democracy and also for the agonies of those who reflect on it. Gatsby has been placed in the middle of a metaphor:

> The most fundamental charge being brought by its critics against New York is the charge that here is an "alien" city, literally un-American and anti-American in its make-up. For this charge does not concern itself with any of the details of New York's alleged hypocrisy, conceit, bare legs, hip-pocket flasks, and Continental morals; it offers, instead, an hypothesis which would explain all of New York on the single central theory that the city has gone foreign.[6]

The writer, Charles Merz, has observed the twenties from the vantage point of *Harper's Magazine*, the *Outlook*, and the *American Sketch*. All these periodicals understand that "foreign" means southern and eastern European. Even more, they understand that it implies American social change. New York is a place, but it is also an idea. For Henry James and others it suggests the devolution of democracy; for Fitzgerald, here and in the stories, it represents quite literally the inherent and necessary kinesis of democracy.

Crowds and democracy have some specific implications in Fitzgerald's text:

1. *Composition:* A percentage of those at Gatsby's party come from the wrong parts of Europe. They have, from the viewpoint of rather a lot of political philosophy, the wrong religion, the wrong political traditions, and almost certainly are first generation. They are quintessentially in business and politics, which are now immigrant avocations. They deal in mass markets like entertainment, which is to say that they circulate among strangers; and they are, in some cases literally, identified with crowds. Another group, like the host, comes from an earlier migration, but members feel the need to translate themselves in class and style. Both groups use the covert instrumentalities of sex and money through marriage.

2. *Aristocracy:* The debate on democracy invariably praised the leavening influence of the patrician minority. That group is visible here, as in endless debates about our

national character and destiny. But the important point in Fitzgerald's catalog is that high and low have met at a destabilizing point. Roughly half of the guests are patrician, the other half plebeian. The former have symbolically lost their identity: even the "name" of a prince called Duke has been "forgotten." Other names have been pretentiously elevated out of the merely democratic condition.[7] Fitzgerald has imaged combinations feared by social philosophy: Santayana, for example, had earlier described the mixed democratic crowd at "their leisure to-day, when a strong aristocratic tradition and the presence of a rich class still profoundly influence popular ideals. Imagine those aristocratic influences removed, and would any head be lifted above a dead level of infinite dulness and vulgarity?"[8] Fitzgerald has in fact imagined it and has made the case more extreme: the aristocracy has not affected the mass but has been absorbed by it. In the process, it has been denatured. Unlike the philosophers, Fitzgerald understands that confusion, especially in the form of sexual mixing, is inevitable. It is important to note that he treats as comedy a social argument that Public Philosophy treats with agonized seriousness.

3. *Continuity*: The essential condition for democracy in 1922 is not the ascription of individual rights but continuity in time. As Walter Lippmann put the matter in that year, the "theory of democracy" is based squarely on a "body of rules" continually retested by those in a particular "community."[9] The ideal is to have both a common

past and a *continuous* sense of self. The person is in part precedent. But one interesting thing about Fitzgerald's description is that some people have so much of the past that they are happy to surrender it. His most ridiculous figures are those from high society who have translated themselves into cafe society. The specifically dated catalog declares itself completely as being in and of the present moment.

4. *Subjectivity:* Edgar Beaver's hair turned cotton white one winter, "for no good reason at all." He is a splendid supernumerary figure, like a carving on a cathedral that implies the promised end. But he is also, and more important, a kind of figure of the ultimate mystery of subjectivity. We will never know why Muldoon strangled his wife or why Henry L. Palmetto jumped in front of a subway train. We will not even learn why Benny McClenahan's girls arrive in sets of four. Many of those at Gatsby's are completely outside the formula for democracy, which necessarily includes objective understanding. Joseph Wood Krutch argued this point with great intensity in his review of this American decade: the great necessities have always been "connections, explanations, and reasons" provided in part by experience, and in part by imagination.[10] Without these things the social order will lose "its patterned completeness." As for this argument, the most fascinating point about Gatsby's world is its absoluteness of self-sufficiency: the background figures are self-referential. They don't have any "commu-

nity" life (they don't, in fact, have any other life that we can detect) because Fitzgerald has made us see them only in terms of announced presence and identity—and, of course, in terms of undisclosed and unreined energies.

In connection with the perils of subjectivity, Krutch observes that the past (he differs here from Royce and William James) consists of beliefs that we may have "to abandon one after another" in the necessary progress toward intellectual maturity.[11] But this admission, I think, is what informs Fitzgerald's understanding of the issue. His novel is about the tensions between our past selves and our new ones. Krutch knows, however, that the surrender of past "experience"—which he opposes to the only resource of the unaided individual, his "imagination"—will be a psychological disaster. "Imagination" of itself cannot confront the "ruthless indifference" of Nature to our desires. And in this too he complements Fitzgerald's understanding.

We can begin to see why Gatsby instinctively invents "ancestors" for his "family tradition" and why Meyer Wolfshiem admires "a man of fine breeding." Neither advocates equality or debates the smell of money. Part of Gatsby's biography comes from current ideas and ideologies of democracy. Literary critics, in trying to explain Gatsby, have often invoked cowboys and pioneers and others with the unlimited imagination of the frontier: he reminds us of Davy Crockett or of those who "set out for gold."[12] But according to Mr. Gatz, "Jimmy always liked it better down East" (131). And Gatsby reminds *himself* of other models: "I am the son of some wealthy people in the middle-west—all dead now. I was brought up in America but educated at Oxford because all my ancestors have been educated there for many years. It is a family tradition" (52). That is to say, he has appropriate democratic-aristocratic connections, clearly a current ideal; his family is rooted in time; there were many (he wisely uses the word "all" several times) propertied ancestors validating his own existential claims. Fitzgerald makes the issue unmistakable when he gives Gatsby *the same terminology that Nick has used for himself*: both men invoke "family" and "tradition" in the same breath. In fact, both are given memories of their "clan." Tocqueville put the matter with his customary acuteness: there are "a thousand continual reminders to every citizen *that he lives in society.*"[13] To identify himself to Nick, Gatsby shows that he "lives in society." Wolfshiem will within a very short time do exactly the same thing. We are reminded, however, of something else: if both Nick and Gatsby use the same language of "clan," "family," and "tradition," then the same ambiguities govern both claims. How much difference is there between a social fiction and a lie?

Immediately after this speech, when Gatsby and Nick drive to New York, the streets they pass contain buildings that are the dark relics of "the faded gilt nineteen-hundreds" (54). The phrase describes urban topography but suggests the rapid disappearance of recent history—the history, in fact, that in the chronology of this novel constitutes biography. The claims of time recently past—what for Fitzgerald was the Victorian past—have no imperative. Even its landscape is dead. The next sentence follows up, contrasting the entropy of this faded past to the "panting vitality" (54) of Myrtle Wilson whose sexual and social energy are clear and uncontainable and present.

Energy and movement are in themselves more meaningful than later readers may think. Fitzgerald has let us know that Gatsby has the quality of "formless grace" expressed by nervous movement and superabundant energy; and that his "restlessness" is "peculiarly American" (51). The last phrase is a guidepost: since Tocqueville, the "restless" character of Americans had been a point of pride and often of alarm, and one of his best-known essays has been "Why the Americans Are Often So Restless in the Midst of Their Prosperity."[14] In this essay Tocqueville asserts that unrest is very nearly metaphysical, directed at the only goals possible in a material and secular social order. It can have grand and even tragic forms: "Men are often less afraid of death than of enduring effort toward one goal."[15] In reaffirming this point, Fitzgerald shares also the contemporary language of democratic debate, which was intensely aware of this attractive and dangerous quality. It gave democracy the fire of individual souls but made universal assent forever impossible. It is very nearly as much of a barrier to ideal democracy as the wrong religion or origin. Fitzgerald is reminiscent of Henry James on this subject, who in *The American Scene* described a form of social character representing not only "the ease, the energy" of New York but its unthinking "restless freedom." (And James thinks also, in this meditation on New York, of the union of the great American realities, nature and science, "joyously romping together" as if impelled by some "collective presence"—although not the mind of God—on New York Bay).[16]

Meyer Wolfshiem occupies a predestined space in the text. He is an assimilated Jew created by an assimilated Catholic who lives in a Protestant society that has not kept faith with its own "ancestors." He is unlike Robert Cohn, the last man aboard the *Titanic,* who has adopted the manner and style and lost illusions of the Protestant ascendancy just at the moment of its disappearance.[17] Wolfshiem has assimilated to the mainstream, and he has its language on his mind: immediately after Gatsby mentions Jordan Baker as being "a great sportswoman," he matches points with the opinion that Gatsby is "a perfect gentleman." Wolfshiem knows the appropriate forms and figures of speech for distance and for intimacy: to have "made the pleasure of his acquaintance just after the war" (57) becomes, the second time around (chapter 9), picking Gatsby up "right out of the gutter" (133). Neither recollection or locution is intended to reach the truth. Having mentioned Oggsford College,

Wolfshiem has obliged himself to imitate its cadences. Later, when he remembers his role in the resurrection of Major Gatsby, he feels compelled to recall the good Samaritan. If we recall Tocqueville on the unreal, inflated rhetoric of democracy, that is really American.

Wolfshiem, like Myrtle Wilson, is convinced that "fine breeding" is necessary (57)—perhaps he too knows that the man on the left in Gatsby's photograph is now the Earl of Doncaster. Furthermore, he knows that there are not many gentleman produced by democracies (it is a highly current theme) and even fewer whom one might want to "take home and introduce to your mother and sister" (57). Wolfshiem may not have "ancestors"—he may not even have a mother and sister—but he knows the demands of social identity. The way to normalize discourse is to claim membership in a world of family and home relationships.

Wolfshiem's position is oddly compromised by those "human molars" (57) he wears for cuff buttons. Nick, who is a bit slow, is driven to think that he may be a dentist, but the reader, a step ahead of him, senses that the idea of relationship has been given a bizarre tilt. The description comes one sentence after Wolfshiem's invocation of motherhood, and one sentence before his solicitous inquiry into Nick's curiosity. The "normal" and the "abnormal" do in fact resist apartness.

The Wolfshiem dialogue invokes words important to the new middle-class media culture. They are not words to be seen in publications like *Vanity Fair*. His language has sources that are not especially concerned with style but that exert high seriousness. They are abstract and moralized. Nothing could be more indicative of class than Wolfshiem's thinking of the past in terms of relationships, and, a few pages later, Jordan Baker's thinking of it in terms of things and styles. Like Myrtle Wilson and Lucille McKee, Wolfshiem seems to begin thought with (not necessarily true) recollection. He talks as if he were in the act of reading the *Saturday Evening Post* about an older man and two younger men meeting in a New York restaurant. The conversation naturally begins with a reference to ladies and gentlemen, proceeds to particulars, defines gentility in the terms of manner and appearance that advertising has assured us is appropriate, and punctuates itself with assembly-line phrases stamped out by the machinery of midcult to assure us that we belong or exist. Gatsby, who "would never so much as look at a friend's wife" (58) might, Nick realizes, in a more recognizable and higher-class language be an exemplar of "instinctive trust." Myrtle Wilson has used these media dreams when she assures us, in language caught in rapid descent from its sources in print, that True Gentility Would Never Countenance George Wilson's Presumption in daring to lick her shoe.

Even clothing ads tell us about "fine breeding," but we can't all have it—although we can act as if the right models for behavior have been memorized. Wolfshiem sticks quite carefully to the moral vocabulary of stage, screen, and newsprint, which seem to be his literary sources: enter stage left, "mother and sister" (57) to prove our bona fides; the idea of friendship is bourgeois-chivalric (we think of Robert Cohn who also got that from the wrong kind of literature); and the duty of "another generation" is to make tolerant way for those who are "young" (58). The reason that Wolfshiem knows about social roles is that he inhabits Broadway, a place that produces them. Before he thinks of Wolfshiem as a dentist, Nick asks, "Who is he anyhow—an actor?" (58). That is to say, he recognizes the social theatricality of the conversation. It has been a kind of script developed from the current annals of the responsible middle class, conscious of family, business, moral trust, and the responsibility we all have to shape our lives not only in a "polite" way but also meaningfully, so as to represent our "generation." *All* of Wolfshiem's subjects are taken very seriously indeed in *Babbitt,* in 1922.

The provincial world of the novel has been caught by Robert Sklar: "The striking image of Jordan Baker's opening paragraph, that when her new plaid skirt blew a little in the wind 'the red, white and blue banners in front of all the houses stretched out stiff and said *tut-tut-tut-tut,* in a disapproving way,' brilliantly conveys the mingled patriotism and prudery of that wartime American society— a society into which, ironically, Jay Gatsby's officer uniform was a sufficient ticket of admission."[18] As Fitzgerald had intuited in his early stories on the disappearing provincial order, nearly everything is now relative. Even in the provinces there are new kinds of valuation.

So far, Jordan has been repeatedly identified as contemptuous, secretive, dishonest, limited, and scornful. Not a happy arrangement for the reader, who has at this point to go through Jordan's longest dialogue and interpret it through her given character. Since this is the only point in the novel in which we find out certain things the case is even harder: we really don't need any more dishonest information. It may be that Jordan's character is in some sense formulated by her own biography—we will never know for sure—but Daisy's character is indelibly inscribed.

Jordan is a more perceptive witness than Nick. She knows what she is seeing—a rarity in this narrative:

> The largest of the banners and the largest of the lawns belonged to Daisy Fay's house. She was just eighteen, two years older than me, and by far the most popular of all the young girls in Louisville. She dressed in white and had a little white roadster and all day long the telephone rang in her house. . . .
>
> When I came opposite her house that morning her white roadster was beside the curb, and she was sitting in it with a lieutenant I had never seen before.

They were so engrossed in each other that she didn't see me until I was five feet away.

"Hello Jordan," she called unexpectedly. "Please come here."

I was flattered that she wanted to speak to me because of all the older girls I admired her most. She asked me if I was going to the Red Cross and make bandages. I was. Well, then, would I tell them that she couldn't come that day? The officer looked at Daisy while she was speaking, in a way that every young girl wants to be looked at sometime, and because it seemed romantic to me I have remembered the incident ever since. [59–60]

About Nick: nothing in his observations about Jordan suggest that she has had this on her mind for five years. It may be that *his* information conveyed to us about her both before and after this statement needs to be qualified. At the least, he is astoundingly imperceptive if she is capable of feeling that way for that long. And at worst, he has dismissed what he does not want to see in her as "dishonesty *in a woman*" (emphasis added), which generalizes away something more real than the words for it, dismissing it with casual sorrow.

About Jordan: to try to be clearheaded and objective about someone richer, more beautiful, more popular, and two years older is difficult, but actually to have done it is to have exceeded the boundaries of complexity. Fitzgerald avoids the relatively handy material of "adolescence," which was another new explanatory word in modern experience: The idea that youth is a stage of life had been available since the turn of century.[19] Although he used that material in his Basil and Josephine stories throughout the twenties, Fitzgerald here pointedly gives Jordan an adult outlook. He does not use circumstances as a way of explaining events and interpretations. This hard-edged narrative is not qualified by Jordan, by the narrator, or by Nick, its immediate audience. We don't hear that she was troubled or envious or that Daisy was typically rebellious. The tone is one of calm acceptance, but the absence of introspection and analysis is meant to be troubling. Jordan voices no regrets and is conspicuously untroubled by provincial sentiment. It does not occur to her to apply moral sentiment of any kind to the story she tells. At what point has she too lost her provincial squeamishness? There is good reason, then, for Daisy to use the phrase "sophisticated" as if it meant shedding the skin of a first life.

About Daisy and Jordan: they are already adult. Daisy makes some decisions about her life, and Jordan makes some observations about facts. Jordan recalls Daisy's status, her own unambiguous involvement, the facts of sexual popularity. Jordan is matter-of-fact about herself—and also about Daisy, whose life is composed of externals: "She dressed in white and had a little white roadster and all day long the telephone rang in her house." But no life is a matter of facts. Jordan's recollection invites interpretations that never appear. Left out is the reason why Jordan is so completely objective, or whether Daisy's white girlhood had anything else in it than has been described. Like the missing clue in the story by Conan Doyle, what matters most here is the absence of curiosity and moral involvement.

Jordan's objectivity is an intentional barrier. When the dialogue continues and she informs us about "wild rumors" about Daisy, she also indicates that she has no inclination to separate them from fact or to interpret Daisy's behavior—or even to be tempted to explain Daisy's being "effectually prevented" (60), from changing her life. Since Jordan accepts all these things, it follows either that she is even more cold-blooded than Nick has suggested—or, since she still remembers "romantic" feelings after five years, that she accepts such things as the norms of social life. Daisy's affair ends with her being "gay again, gay as ever" (60), a description with as many layers as there are skins on an onion. One imagines that gaiety is a conscious choice. It may involve internal penalties, but again Jordan has nothing to say about that. It is meant, I think, to reverberate with Nick's previous observations about Daisy, to fill them in and make them more contextual. There are reasons for her theatricality. Jordan knows everything she needs to but is rationally incurious about it. What she sees, evidently, is simply a working out of what she expects to see. And if that is true, what she sees is the way things are, which is not what Nick or other men in the story see.

Nick has already told us that the Buchanan wealth is excessive—perhaps monstrous—but when Jordan describes it, she leaves out anything morally or psychologically connotative. Four private railroad cars and a necklace worth several lifetimes of wage earning may easily irritate the virtuous but draw no blood from her. Jordan accepts Daisy's getting drunk, the wedding, Daisy's falling in love with Tom, Tom with "one of the chambermaids," and Daisy's later moving with "a fast crowd" (61). This calm negativity is one of the most interesting things about Jordan.

Jordan is "fascinated" by seeing emotions that, possibly, she herself does not experience. Her description of Daisy—"But she didn't say another word" (61)—is also self-description. Most of the information she gives us is interesting because it is stated without being thought or felt. Somewhere between the character gained from insight, experience, and necessity and that enforced by some undisclosed internal strategy is the truth about both of them. But we are not going to get it.

Jordan may enjoy seeing things that others may be "blind" to—she is telling her own story through Daisy's. We presume that she has certain ideas about their white girlhood; about the *particulars* of love of "a girl so mad about her husband" (61) (in itself able to constitute a story) and about *her own* overriding problem, that of "reputation." She releases much psychological information about herself when she talks about someone else. Jordan has a good, cold mind that appears to Nick to be "limited" but is more complicated. It looks as if she knows everything she needs to know but doesn't want to know anymore. And like Daisy, she doesn't want anyone else to know her. The first, untouchable image of the two of them at the Buchanan's may be their defining image. All evocations by Nick and Gatsby and Wolfshiem (and Tom Buchanan) of the norms of life seem to have left these women out. They are dealing with the same materials—family, home, community, relationship—but it turns out that, when viewed "objectively," these things don't exist. The feelings are there, and a woman can be "mad" about her husband, but the forms don't answer to the feelings. We tend not to remember that by the end of the story Jordan, who is here only clean, hard, limited, and skeptical, becomes "wise." Her life, like Daisy's, is composed of externals because they are much easier to deal with. Few explanations are wanted in their lives.

◄5►

Individualism Reconsidered

In chapter 4 of *The Great Gatsby* Fitzgerald broached Gatsby's "restlessness," which "was continually breaking through his punctilious manner" (51). The quality of unrest is important to Fitzgerald, and he evokes it again in the fifth chapter, beginning with the explosion of lights at Gatsby's house "lit from tower to cellar" (64), indicating the passage of his thought. Gatsby has been walking through his recreated life, going from room to room to assure himself of what he is. Nick is sensible enough to want at two o'clock in the morning to go to bed, but Gatsby, overflowing with energies, wants to go to Coney Island, take a swim, arrange for the grass to be cut, make a deal with Nick, get ready for Daisy's visit. The house blazes on all night, as if the whole peninsula is on fire. The scene externalizes feeling, makes Gatsby's vital energies visible. Its language is compelling and cast in familiar terms. Fitzgerald had already equated fire and sensibility. Among his early attempts at both poetry and prose are these lines recycled by *This Side of Paradise:* "Here, Heraclitus, did you find in fire and shifting things the prophecy you hurled down the dead years; this midnight my desire will see, shadowed among the embers, furled in flame, the splendor and the sadness of the world."[1]

In a letter to his daughter Fitzgerald wrote that poetry or imagination itself "lives like fire inside you." He was referring to Keats and his value "for anybody who wants truly to know about words."[2] But light and fire are also part of a poetic continuum that goes past romanticism: "fire itself, or comparisons of things to fire, forms a remarkable pattern of association, all centering around the theme of heroic passion and death."[3] These comparisons are essential to epic, a genre with conscious echoes here. The combination of erotic feeling and heroism is Vergilian rather than Homeric.

The fifth chapter must have been difficult to put together. It tries to deploy an idea of Americanism, literary history, and the exigencies of plot. As to the first, Fitzgerald had been thinking about American unrest for some time—in 1920 he wrote about it as a more than metabolic quality. The subsection "Restlessness" in *This Side of Paradise* states at length what this "peculiarly American" quality means. Amory Blaine is arguing the meaning of national character among the new masses. He has in mind the newspaper-reading literate and educated—the herd of independent minds. There is a national disease of words, and they have dissolved the possibilities of heroism in political life:

> "You're mistaking this period when every nut is an individualist for a period of individualism. Wilson has only been powerful when he has represented; he's had to compromise over and over again. . . . Even Foch hasn't half the significance of Stonewall Jackson. . . .
>
> "Then you don't think there will be any more permanent world heroes?"
>
> "Yes—in history—not in life. Carlyle would have difficulty getting material for a new chapter on 'The Hero as a Big Man.'"
>
> "Go on. I'm a good listener to-day."
>
> "People try so hard to believe in leaders now, pitifully hard. But we no sooner get a popular reformer or politician or soldier or writer or philosopher—a Roosevelt, a Tolstoi, a Wood, a Shaw, A Nietzsche, than the cross-currents of criticism wash him away. . . .
>
> "We *want* to believe. Young students try to believe in older authors, constituents try to believe in their Congressmen, countries try to believe in their statesmen, but they *can't*. Too many voices, too much scattered, illogical, ill-considered criticism.[4]

Or as James stated, "thousands of innocent magazine readers lie paralyzed and terrified in the network of shallow negations which the leaders of opinion have thrown over their souls."[5] As far as Fitzgerald is concerned, both war and politics, the conventional modes of greatness, have been removed from consideration, leaving only the private realm for the energies of engagement. There has in fact been a tremendous split between the private and the public realms, so that the latter is no longer imaginatively attractive. The hero who represents a public ideal is as little possible for Fitzgerald as for Hemingway. There are themes here waiting to be worked out: the necessity of individualism; its existential and not necessarily moral heroism; the understood opposition of old and young, which is a form of *ressentiment* in Fitzgerald. "Restlessness" sets us apart from the ordinary and gives us insight into something higher than that. It is, very nearly by definition, tremendously sexual—the native property of youth. And it is heroic, although in a way significantly different from conventional example or literary history. Amory Blaine has not thought his ideas out completely— the conclusion of his dialogue may be as much Fitzgerald's as his, waiting for a novel large enough to contain them: "I have sworn not to put pen to paper until my ideas either clarify or depart entirely."[6]

Amory Blaine may be superficial, but he is right: according to Hannah Arendt in *The Human Condition,* the larger the population of any polity, and the more complex its arrangements, the more likely social issues are to replace political issues. A real sense of polity disappears— as in "the modern age," her specific example—leading to "conformism, behaviorism, and automatism in human affairs." We are less likely to witness "rare deeds," more likely to be "submerged in the routine of everyday living," and more compelled to think like the socialized herd.[7]

We ought at this point to think about that word *great* used by James, by Lippmann, and from time to time by Fitzgerald. For one thing, it no longer refers automatically to national ideas. Greatness has been separated from its largest connection. Perhaps the issue has best been described by W. H. Auden, who brought it up to date when, like Fitzgerald, he began to think about modern conditions. In *The Dyer's Hand* Auden writes that we have witnessed "the disappearance of the Public Realm as the sphere of revelatory personal deeds." Our former idol, "the man of action," can only act now in his personal life—it is not even a possibility for him to be a public figure. Like Fitzgerald and certainly like Hannah Arendt, Auden connects this limitation to mob and to media— and both to the extinction of the ideal of greatness. The crowd is passively unwilling to recognize greatness because the quality is offensively uncommon; while the media are actively hostile to greatness because the quality resists "entertainment."[8] As Fitzgerald put the matter in 1920, public or political greatness is visible only in history. Hence the movement in Fitzgerald, as in American idealism in general, away from political life, and toward existential heroism. But every time the word is used in *The Great Gatsby* we are intended to see a large and political irony. Succeeding chapters will develop the conflict with ever-greater specificity.

Those named by Amory Blaine throw off waves of psychic energy. Shaw believed that vitality, Gatsby's defining quality, was the essential for social life. He associated vitality with existential heroism. Shaw's Caesar, for example, is not only a world-political figure but "sheer vitality incarnate for the moment."[9] Shaw's Saint Joan had appeared in 1923, just before *Gatsby,* to announce that she was about "God's business" here on earth.[10] Fitzgerald may not have been above borrowing the phrase. She prefigures the feared "energy" of the true individual who changes our moral boundaries against our will.[11] Hence her interlocutor asks, like the rest of us, only not to have courage put into him.

From Sally Carrol Happer in "The Ice Palace" (1920), who knows that she is "restless" and has a civilizing "energy" that can be "useful" to society, to those "nervous" energies spilt by George O'Kelly in "The Sensible Thing" (1924), to Gatsby's own "nervous" grace, to the "generosities" of American "excess" intuited by Henry Marston in "The Swimmers" (1929), the vital spirit of the whole infuses chosen individuals. But this national spirit is oft defeated.

Public Philosophy had long established the national sense of opposition between passivity, self-love, and lethargy (qualities that William James stated were characteristic of the inertia of gentility) and something far bet-

ter, "the instinctive springs of vitality" that mere civilization and American history have lost.[12] James preached
"the old heights and depths and romantic chiaroscuro
. . . , higher heroisms and the old rare flavors . . . , passing
out of life."[13] Much as he hoped for the moral consequences of passion and the risk of action, James knew
that from the world of the Chautauqua to that of the
new college-educated middle classes, few would agree. It
might be, James said with mordant wit, that romantic
heroism could only be displayed through a life of crime—
which might be an improvement on mere blamelessness.
He was joking but not too far off the mark. In the following generation the American marketplace would become
saturated with stories and silent movies about the last
heroes left on earth, Robin Hood and Raffles and Arsène
Lupin and the Thief of Baghdad who alone could express
a sense of self that civilization was busy strangling. The
audience for these stories included Basil Lee, who in
"The Freshest Boy" dreams of Broadway and (an idea that
resurfaces in *The Great Gatsby*) dominating "the under-
world." In "The Scandal Detectives" Basil longs hopelessly to become a "gentleman burglar"—seeking, like
James, something more "primordial" than civilized self-
satisfaction.

James was a Founding Father of the active life who
preached that "*excitements, ideas, and efforts* . . . are what
carry us over the dam."[14] More important, James linked
"energies" with "ideas." He stated plainly that "certain

ideas naturally awaken the energies of loyalty, courage, endurance, or devotion." Their unsuspected effect, he added, is "often very great indeed."[15] James, like Fitzgerald, recognizes that "the heroes and heroines of Bernard Shaw" express the "vitality" of human feelings.[16] He adds to his list of authorities on vital individualism (as in the lists of *This Side of Paradise*), G. K. Chesterton and H. G. Wells. To give off energies is to have the capacity for moral action, an idea that Nick Carraway inherits. But what of the ends of action? And its effects planned and unplanned?

In "The Dilemma of Determinism" James developed two important points, the first copiously illustrated by lines from Omar Khayyam: our duty to change the nature of things and remake them "nearer to the Heart's Desire." This duty called for grand and even romantic energies working against that which seemed to be incontrovertible social order but was in reality only the mere inertia of habit and custom. In that sense, James was decidedly anti-Victorian. Important as this stance is for understanding both James and Fitzgerald, it may be more critical to remember that subjectivism, which could also derive from romantic feeling, might be mere unthinking self-assertion. It might well result in "nerveless sentimentality," stupid optimism, and final indifference to things and people. It was useless, James argued, to possess sensibility without limits and without a real subject outside the self.[17] The expression of nervous energy was a sign of moral capability, but the form it needed to take was that of dedication to a cause.

The opposite of the vital individual is not the mass man or woman; it is the false individualist. Replicated individuals, under the impression that they are each different, in fact imitate each other and compose the mass. Hannah Arendt states that their values, naturally, are those of self-interest; and that such "individuals" become entirely self-referential. They develop a "life philosophy in its most vulgar and least critical form."[18] It will always justify itself by reference to *their* lives. There are moments in the text of *The Great Gatsby* that Arendt can clarify. When Jordan Baker finishes her story she says to Nick, "And Daisy ought to have something in her life" (63). The words "Daisy" and "life" seem like ordinary referents, but they silently state that whatever is outside them is simply ancillary. To have "something" is to call into being antithetical possibilities: it is as if Daisy had nothing, while she has had very nearly everything. In a comparable moment Catherine says of her sister Myrtle, "They've been living over that garage for eleven years. And Tom's the first sweetie she ever had" (30). Catherine and Jordan may well be right—Myrtle and Daisy, in fact, may well be right—but the argument for love and freedom has become, as Hannah Arendt puts it, life philosophy in its most vulgar and least critical form. The issue is the reduction of all other meanings to self. This is as important as the opposition of classes.

Fitzgerald has made Gatsby much less self-referential than the cast surrounding him. Myrtle Wilson uses the word "I" more than anyone else—it is the understood opening of nearly every sentence and the introduction of each observation. She will use the word a great many times among other words as if it were an understood modifier: " 'Oh, is that your suit?' I said. 'This is the first I ever heard about it.' But I gave it to him and then I lay down and cried to beat the band all afternoon" (30). Daisy too feels impelled to define by saying, "let me tell you what I said. . . . I think everything's terrible anyhow" (17). Subjectivity gone soft is a kind of *argument* in the narrative. It brings to dialogue the understood assumption that the person expressing it has a "life philosophy" proceeding from the debt owed that person by all else and all others. As Arendt points out, it means that the only moral standard is a happy continuation. The locutions I've cited are part of the fake "individualist" argument that Fitzgerald began to identify in *This Side of Paradise* in 1920. It is a decent argument for a writer to make who has been accused of being a lightweight; he understands how mind confuses solipsism with individuality and how language expresses that confusion.

Gatsby is by no means immune: when he is most false he indicates most reliance on the language he has derived from the marketplace. His conversation with Nick about Oxford and Venice and Rome is punctuated with self-reference—although the saving distinction is that "I" is a form of location. He does not define meanings by proceeding from a pronoun. In fact, he will reverse what is coming to be a normal expectation: when Nick and Gatsby discuss inviting Daisy, Gatsby shows a kind of linguistic noblesse oblige in the shifting of pronouns. The text makes its own emphasis:

> "What day would suit you?"
> "What day would suit *you?*" he corrected me quickly. "I don't want to put you to any trouble, you see." [64]

This manner may be derived, and even false, but his mind models its information in this way. He is generally conscious about not stating mere subjective imperatives. He is in the service of necessity.

Gatsby has difficulties that are derived from the marketplace, and they intrude, in this chapter about the energies of love, in ways that we are forced to recognize:

> "There's another little thing," he said uncertainly, and hesitated.
> "Would you rather put it off a few days?" I asked.
> "Oh, it isn't about that. At least——" He fumbled with a series of beginnings. "Why, I thought—why, look here, old sport, you don't make much money, do you?"

"Not very much."

This seemed to reassure him, and he continued more confidently.

"I thought you didn't, if you'll pardon my—you see, I carry on a little business on the side, a sort of a sideline, you understand. And I thought that if you don't make very much——You're selling bonds, aren't you, old sport?" [65]

The hesitancy becomes clear when we think about what "business" means and why Gatsby adds, "You wouldn't have to do any business with Wolfsheim." Gatsby is being literary-honorable, imitating the gentry he has read about in magazines or those whom he has briefly known at Oxford, to whom any business would indeed be a sideline. Gatsby's "business" reality is getting or extorting money. He thinks about this activity, or rather avoids thinking about it, saying first that his money has been inherited and second (more honest and less rehearsed) that it has been earned. There are two fictions here: he is lying not only to Nick but to himself. Gatsby aspires to Anglophile leisure, an idea that comes to him not from the American West but from all of those magazines whose ads swoon over plus fours and British golfing shoes and mackintoshes and the latest tweeds of the Prince of Wales (who is the subject of one of Fitzgerald's social fantasies).[19] The mention of mere money is itself destabilizing to such a view of self (and shows how far Tom Buchanan has fallen in his dealings with Wilson). But Nick, who really is to the manner born, understands that it is not the money but the mention: he does not deal in services to be rendered.

Gatsby is unable to think why Nick turns him down, guessing only that it has to do with his natural reluctance—a compound of good taste and conventional anti-Semitism—"to do any business with Wolfsheim" (65). He shares these things, or the idea of these things, but is too naive to realize that "business" is for Nick part of a different order of things. Whatever the Carraways may have has proceeded from "the wholesale hardware business that my father carries on today" (6). They have for some time been trying to wash away the curse of its origin and, we gather from the novel's opening, talk a good deal more about the righteous bourgeois style than about profit and loss. Nick is skeptical about both: the style is not, so far as he can see, particularly attractive or even believable, and he has more on his mind than either manufactured tradition or money. Wolfsheim, however, thinks of business as an entry to Babbitt-America, a "business gonnegtion" (56) that allows complacent self-regard and even social self-invention. It is one of the ways in which he is "sentimental." In that, he is like Chauncey M. Depew, an icon of the past age, whose earnest muttonchops adorn a full-page ad in the first issue (February 21, 1925) of the *New Yorker,* which came out shortly before the publication of *The Great Gatsby.* Depew thinks back to those

loyal and "whole hearts" who presented him with an El-
gin watch upon retirement—and of the "tears at the part-
ing of our association." It is a form of sentimentality that
the historically minded and alert Wolfsheim knows is on
the way out. Depew will be replaced by some film star
who will sell more watches through the appeal to glamor
than could ever have been sold through this antiquated
business style based on value and values. Gatsby's ideas
will also be replaced. His view of "business" is leisure-
class British, transmitted by novels like those of Comp-
ton Mackenzie, compounded by advice to consumers
from middle-class magazine culture. Since the decline of
the pound and the Empire, economists have noted that
those who aspire to do "a little business on the side" (65)
from their landed estates have fatally misunderstood
the marketplace. In their different ways, Wolfsheim and
Gatsby believe that "business" is redemptive, and in their
different ways they are wrong.

There is another gargoyle on Fitzgerald's cathedral,
the disappointed brewer who built Gatsby's castle a decade before and who died after his neighbors refused to
reify his social dream. He too has come from the world
of "business" success only to find out the limits of change.
His career and his ending mimic some of the main
themes of the narrative:

There was nothing to look at from under the tree except Gatsby's enormous house so I stared at it, like

Kant at his church steeple, for half an hour. A brewer had built it early in the "period" craze, a decade before, and there was a story that he'd agreed to pay five years' taxes on all the neighboring cottages if the owners would have their roofs thatched with straw. Perhaps their refusal took the heart out of his plan to Found a Family—he went into an immediate decline. His children sold his house with the black wreath still on the door. Americans, while occasionally willing to be serfs, have always been obstinate about being peasantry. [69]

The story is, as Nick emphasizes, an American story. Tocqueville had forecast the conflict of money and class: "Among democratic peoples men easily obtain a certain equality, but they will never get the sort of equality they long for. . . . and they will be dead before they have fully relished its delights."[20] There are a number of reasons, among them the innate hostilities of equality and the limits of distinction available under democracy. Fitzgerald's brewer hopes for transcendence of his condition, believing that he too can put his dreams into objective, landed—and anglicized—form. Such dreams are of special interest because they imitate Gatsby's own quest for appropriate style and condition and mock the quest for that democratic aristocracy so much admired by political philosophy and the protagonists of this novel.[21] The text states that the quest is by now a hopeless crux: we live not in an aristocracy but in a plutocracy. Like Gatsby (and, certainly, like Tom Buchanan), the obsessed brewer thinks not of pioneer equality but of Edwardian prerogative. Words like "ancestors" and "gentleman" and "Family" refer to an open debate on democracy. We may need a counterbalance to the masses—but it is too late for that to happen, except in the realm of social style, an idea inherently comic.

The facts remain: like Tom's place, Gatsby's "enormous house" is a commodity in transition between temporary owners. It is America itself. Fitzgerald's narrative has epicycles, an orbit of smaller sketches, histories, and biographies that refer in a seemingly unconscious way to the main thing. In this case a national truism is revealed by the brewer's swift decline and the instantaneous imposition of marketplace laws ("His children sold his house with the black wreath still on the door") over the imperatives of his dream. The result is a quick sale and a quick forgetting, the last of which really is a great American theme.

The text balances the mundane against the eternal. On a scale of high poetic seriousness, it alludes to Ovidian transmutation, and to Vergilian moments, but it has other ways of stating its subject. Below transmutation—and at a considerable spiritual distance—is its gross and earthly form, social mobility. The hopeful brewer brings to the story expectations of change through success. As Fitzgerald's audience knows, the brewer's story is not just about silk purses and sows' ears. The American lives that enter the text tell about the defeat of metamorphosis: from the plangent biographies of Lucille McKee and Myrtle Wilson to the elegy for a millionaire brewer from West Egg. The wish for imaginative change—which means the control of destiny—is often restated. When Ewing Klipspringer plays "The Love Nest" for Gatsby and Daisy (from the musical *Mary,* 1920), he brings into the text not only the music and lyrics of Broadway but the tensions of American history as well. This number is about a man and a woman in a place called "home." It is nothing like the place in which the song is being played. The lyrics of *Mary* are about "a love nest" impossibly distant: Klipspringer plays for the Broadway audience of 1922 a song about love down on the farm. The feelings are those of a vanishing American past. Love here, in a small kitchen covered with roses is "better than a palace." It is love forever—married love, and with not much money or use for it.[22]

The song calls for feelings a generation out of date, which is part of its appeal for Broadway. It is not only about marriage without money, but faith without end. In Gatsby's palace we hear about an American dream that has already run its course. Throughout the book we are forced to alter time, place, and location in our minds. Here the city dreams of the country, entertains itself with impossible innocence. The text makes its allusions in a minor key because they tell us about Gatsby's story in diminished form. The great subject of the Jazz Age, money, is conspicuous by its imaginative absence. These lyrics, about moral simplicity, shade the novel's complexities: not only is money absent but class as well. As for "home," that idea gets one more redefinition as a place unreal. Perhaps of a country unreal.

After Max Perkins read the manuscript of *The Great Gatsby* and wrote his splendid letter about it, he received a response from Fitzgerald: "Your criticisms were excellent & most helpful & you picked out all my favorite spots in the book to praise as high spots. Except you didn't mention my favorite of all—the chapter where Gatsby & Daisy meet."[23] There is more than one kind of reality in this part of the book.

Fitzgerald has made it rain for us to see Daisy in an open car:

> The exhilarating ripple of her voice was a wild tonic in the rain. I had to follow the sound of it for a moment, up and down, with my ear alone before any words came through. A damp streak of hair lay like a dash of blue paint across her cheek and her hand was wet with glistening drops as I took it to help her from the car.
>
> "Are you in love with me?" she said low in my ear.
> "Or why did I have to come alone?" [67]

She is quite right—Nick is in love with her, as most should be who read the passage. Daisy is in another incarnation; the goddess who moves through the universe "with the season" (118) is *dea certa,* come to earth in the element. We see her at evening and dawn—Dryden's translation of Vergil calls her "the Sister of the Day" and asks whether a stranger can call her name, be her suppliant. Part she grants, but Venus lives in "borrow'd Shapes" and disappears from those who love her. When she descends, Dryden writes, she has "dishevel'd Hair."[24] Fitzgerald's recollection isn't too bad, given that he hated literature at Princeton and failed the Latin exam twice.[25] There is, however, more to Fitzgerald's classicizing.

The rain is real, but it is also literary, an answer to the dry and sterile Waste Land that Fitzgerald has appropriated. And it is part of another conception:

> When I came home to West Egg that night I was afraid for a moment that my house was on fire. Two o'clock and the whole corner of the peninsula was blazing with light. [64]

> A huge black knotted tree. . . . small muddy swamps and prehistoric marshes. [69]

> Aware of the loud beating of my own heart I pulled the door to against the increasing rain. [68]

> All the lights were going on in West Egg now; the electric trains, men-carrying, were plunging home

through the rain from New York. It was the hour of a
profound human change and excitement was generat-
ing on the air. [75]

For transmutation to occur we need and the text provides
a world of fire and water, earth and air. The meter is no
longer iambic and phrases like "men-carrying" insist on a
different kind of reading, rhythm, and allusiveness.
When Fitzgerald left for France in summer 1924, he
wrote, "I'm going to read nothing but Homer & Homeric
literature—and history 540–1200 A.D. until I finish my
novel."[26] He clearly associated epic with a certain kind of
feeling and that feeling with his story.

One of the great accomplishments of this chapter is
its intellectual play with a sequence that goes from
change to transmutation. At the beginning of the episode,
Gatsby becomes larger than life because he brings to it
the heroic quality of vital energy. Like Saint Joan he is a
paragon of ignorance—and, in a certain way, of innocence. His story too deals with betrayal. But as the episode develops, Fitzgerald persuades us of something as
Shaw never could, that there really is a mythological quality to life and that we can't reach it by unremitting social
analysis. Daisy is neither good nor evil but also a "Life-
Force." When the goddesses come to earth, it is no use
moralizing about what they do. And when they leave, the
goddesses turn away their eyes, as they have for a long
time been telling us.[27] Or as Fitzgerald put it of another

of his incarnations, Miss Erminie Gilberte Labouisse Bibble, also known as Cleopatra, "she scarcely perceived him; he was a lay figure."[28] But she is his cause.

Between epic and history: in one sense, and it is an important sense, Gatsby's "colossal vitality" and "passion" are political qualities. A very modern mind, that of Harold E. Stearns, reflected in 1922 that the "germinal energies" for a good national life came directly from the "passions" and opposed the style of mere decency.[29] The reformist Stearns might almost have had in view the eventual triumph of Buchananism, or, another alternative, of Babbitry. He might almost have been hoping, in 1922, for the appearance of something very like Gatsby.

6

Energies

Jay Gatsby was born Jimmy Gatz around 1890 to shiftless dirt farmers who gave him a past to forget. Thereafter the stages of his life form both a chronology and a reading list. In 1906, in the last flyleaf of a text important to him, "Hopalong Cassidy" (actual date of publication 1910), he enters thoughts about reading and the good life. The self-admonition of going through "one improving book or magazine per week" is connected to "Work," "poise," and being "better to parents" (135). It is a list of rural commandments, designed around not only utilitarian virtues but also a sense of national character. His regimen has led infallibly, his father knows, to "success" and would have resulted in his becoming "a great man" who would "of helped build up the country" (131). That phrase "great man" is important and will be widely intertextual from 1906 to 1922. Greatness is not simply personal; it has public shape and conscious-ness.

About a year later, approximately 1907, Jimmy Gatz runs away from home and becomes Jay Gatsby. He has lived the life of a roughneck while developing concep-tions from somewhere about all the beauty and glamor in the world. But while living with Dan Cody he refuses Dan Cody's life. He is governed by certain standards that make his life Talmudic, a series of negative observances that are important for us to grasp. We don't know where he gets his restraint (although it is a Conradian quality), but it will be important to sense that part of him. Gatsby stays away from what most men pursue, resembling other literary heroes of self-change and discipline from Shake-speare's new Adam, Henry V, to George Bernard Shaw's Caesar. The first measure of his new life is self-control. In that he will be set against other distinctively American heroes who take the road of excess to no particular des-tination.

Having received two kinds of education, he enters another stage of biography and identity. In Louisville, at war, and at Oxford he is accepted as an officer and a gentleman. There is proof positive in 1919: Wolfsheim, who notices these things, recalls that even in trouble Gatsby was "a fine appearing gentlemanly young man" (133). This time, in a complementary way, the emphasis is on externals. They have proceeded from something internal. Manner itself is derived from an idea of restraint that lies behind the idea of being a gentleman.

When Gatsby sums up his own life in 1922 he adds another component derived from many "magazines." Gatsby mentions a number of newsstand themes, among them hunting big game and experiencing epical sadness over lost love. Again, there are the complementary themes of internal sensibility and the mastery of external style. From 1906 to 1922 Gatsby has recreated himself a number of times. Each incarnation not only is a form of fiction but is inspired by fictions for sale. And his "rise," of course, is itself an imitation of a very popular form of fiction on the American scene.

The idea of greatness has, meanwhile, itself undergone a change. The magazines that Nick has recognized (in chapter 4) don't have much to say about actually *working* for greatness. The tactics of day-to-day labor are familiar, but they seem no longer to be interesting. Even Fitzgerald honors the idea of "success" through work more in the breach than in the observance. His heroes depart from the scene, then simply return with their fortunes to tell us where they have been. It might be interesting to learn how money is made in the laundries and drugstores and mines that he mentions—but Fitzgerald's concern does not lie in telling us.

Gatsby's actual biography is more interesting than the one he invents; it is, after all, a retelling of a national story about log-cabin lives. Much feeling already attaches to this story in American history. But Gatsby seems to recognize that it is no longer imaginatively compelling. That story has been hopelessly dated. The creation and fostering of personality seem to have replaced the embodiment of earnestness. We are now interested less in *rising* than in *changing,* so that one kind of romance has replaced another. I don't mean the kind of change that comes about from the polishing effect of success, the frictional removal of burrs and callouses as hard hands get soft. The idea of change has by 1922 become a dream of new selfhood, really of metamorphosis.

It is important to remain aware that Gatsby's real story is part of democratic mythology. It is rural and proletarian and infused with public ideals. It says a great deal that his life becomes ever more intensely private and that the ideals he begins with, which are prairie American, are replaced by a mythology of a certain style, manner, and status. Fitzgerald has brought the "real" story to textual life, then submerged it under a replacing story that is in many ways its inferior. The two stories have an adversary relationship. They ask us to compare them and to compare our attitudes about them.

Do we prefer the new story to the real one? Gatsby, evidently, prefers the former and wastes no recollection on the latter. But Nick, in the way that he describes the old story, just as clearly establishes his own preferences. He marvels at the real changes in Gatsby's life and knows that the qualities they displayed were substantial. Gatsby's real life has been at least as adventurous as the fiction he has relied on to invent his "unreal" life. And it has called for a kind of sophistication that newsstand models of identity (which have become our models of identity) fail completely to understand.

Gatsby wants to be a "great man," and this ambition has for long been an American theme. But his first conception of greatness will itself be transformed. Even for the newer and more personal idea of greatness there will be many obstacles. Not all of them are interposed by the indifference of "destiny"—the difficulty in achieving greatness is that it seems to be a quality without much marketplace value. In 1919 the starving hero is lifted out of a gutter, which is a satirical enough way of restating a point already made by Kipling. In 1922 Gatsby's epical devotion is incapable of being understood and will at his symbolic funeral be forgotten by his own "public." Gatsby's greatness will be set not only against the moral Lilliputians he encounters but against some new American realities.

The sixth chapter, decisively, starts with a description of journalism and its persistent misunderstanding of things human. There are some probable reasons for this emphasis on the "news," chief among them Fitzgerald's sense that it represents coerced common judgment. He was, I think, aware that by evoking newspapers, magazines, and their influence on the imagination he was participating in a current debate. To write about newsstand fictions of identity in the year 1922 was to state the point even more strongly, because in that year, the year of Fitzgerald's narrative, the Public Philosophy had been heavily reinforced. William James's ideas about the way Americans saw and understood themselves underpinned Walter Lippmann's thesis in *Public Opinion:* by 1922 most Americans were plainly deriving their sense of self from the consumer culture and, within it, from the popular press. Josiah Royce had stated that it would become possible to choose what part of the self would be abandoned; and William James knew that selfhood might be achieved—purchased—from models of media. There would not be much greatness about it.

Gatsby's troubles begin when a reporter appears to investigate stories that even a novelist might not imagine: Gatsby evidently inhabits "a boat that looked like a house and was moved secretly up and down the Long Island shore (76), a fact that is even more improbable than that he is Kaiser Wilhelm's cousin. Fitzgerald excoriates the "news" that saturates public imagination with "contemporary legends" (76). He shares the theme with Lippmann, whose *Public Opinion* begins with an examination of fake biography and history from the newsstand: "Great men, even during their lifetime, are usually known to the public only through a fictitious personality."[1] But two years before Lippmann's book had appeared, in 1920, Fitzgerald had identified what *he* thought were the prime causes of the decline of "great men" (his own anticipatory phrase) in America: "It's worse in the case of newspapers."[2] It is not only that the "ambitious" reporter has no mind to speak of—within a very few pages we will hear of Ella Kaye, "the newspaper woman" (78), who reenacts the fundamental crime of betrayal. She could, we suppose, have been given any conceivable other kind of identity herself. But she takes on the identity of those who "expose" or reduce beliefs and ideals. Greatness and journalism cannot be reconciled: and journalism (later described as "grotesque, circumstantial, eager and untrue" [127]) is the representative quality, the actual sign, of the cultural moment and its mind. Its figures (reporters, photographers, avid readers) remind us that it has a case against greatness, and so do we. The idea of greatness is, in 1922, made less conceivable and more suspect; current sensibility clearly cannot afford to tolerate such an idea.

When Lippmann writes about "news," he, like Fitzgerald, does more than invoke commercial dishonesty. He recognizes the fragility of the construction of reality. And he thinks of journalism as a dissolvent of a "human culture" that "is very largely the selection, the rearrangement, the tracing of patterns upon, and the stylizing of, what William James called 'the random irradiations and resettlements of our ideas.' "[3] Lippmann is irritated by sentimentalism and fakery: what we too readily call "news" suppresses the actual facts and ignores the real "ebb and flow of sensation." It becomes a desirable commodity because it is untrue. We want to simplify, to think in "codes" and about "stereotypes." Those members of the public who rely for their information on the lowest-common-denominator press are like those who misjudge Gatsby (and, we gather, inescapably, they are like Gatsby himself): "the pictures inside people's heads do not automatically correspond with the world outside."[4] Mass citizenship does not understand things outside itself.

Fitzgerald is more concerned with the specific issue of getting ideas of selfhood from the newsstand as Tom, Myrtle, Daisy, and Gatsby do. All have obtained much more than "news" from magazines and newspapers, from ads, illustrations, and twice-told consumer tales. Nick has already stated that a likely "dozen" magazines have given Gatsby his biography with its retail weltschmerz. Later we will find that in his caterpillar stage, as Jimmy Gatz, he has depended on other kinds of journalism for the disguises of identity.

We may not know which "improving" magazines Jimmy Gatz had in mind in 1906, but William James knew some of them in 1907. His address at Radcliffe, "The Social Value of the College-Bred," discusses not only the "improving" of the national self but new models for its construction:

McClure's Magazine, the American Magazine, Collier's Weekly, and, in its fashion, the World's Work, constitute together a real popular university. . . . It would be a pity if any future historian were to have to write words like these: "By the middle of the twentieth century the higher institutions of learning had lost all influence over public opinion in the United States. But the mission of raising the tone of democracy, which they had proved themselves so lamentably unfitted to exert, was assumed with rare enthusiasm and prosecuted with extraordinary skill and success by a new educational power; and for the clarification of their human sympathies and elevation of their human preferences, the people at large acquired the habit of resorting exclusively to the guidance of certain private literary adventures, commonly designated in the market by the affectionate name of ten-cent magazines."[5]

What ideas might a provincial reader have picked up from the mass market of improvement? To judge from Jimmy Gatz, and from Mr. Gatz, personal success was part of national success. To better yourself was to reenact the national experience of economic and hence moral growth. James mentions *The World's Work,* a magazine that relentlessly stated that the creation of wealth was "the product of our national genius"—and a certain proof of our national honor (June 1906, 7066). Mr. Gatz, better informed than he seems to be, knows that we "build up the country" by getting rich. *The World's Work* agrees: "by building up the country" (7071) great rich men justify their lives and make *our* lives better. *Collier's* is much more critical of achieved wealth, but the lead editorial of April 29, 1905, mourns those "great figures" who have become rare in America as heroic individualism subsides (9). Throughout the spring issues of 1905 it recalls the idea of the true businessman-hero whose own success should be a model for that of everyone else.

Fitzgerald, however, sees more than one irony in the relationship between national character, novelistic characters, and the texts of mass literacy and "preferences." James may have foreseen the failure of the higher "influence" on American lives, but it did not take until midcentury for the American imagination to become dependent on mass image and print. Within two decades *The Great Gatsby* illustrated in detail the cumulative effects of mass marketing on the construction of identity. The magazines that Fitzgerald mentions now educate in a different way. He is deeply attentive to derived language and idea and makes explicit connections between what characters think (and how they say what they think) and what they read. And in his own text, he shows the presence of deconstructive journalistic intelligence that refuses to take seriously the story that we are asked to take seriously. In Fitzgerald, the press is a mordant figure for the adversaries of art and imagination. Magazines are mindless, best-sellers can be racist. The reductive and "turgid" journalism of 1902 differs little from that of autumn 1922. The "endless" swarm of reporters and journalists pursuing Gatsby's death not only is ghoulish in itself but rivals the telling of truth by writing. At particular points in the text Fitzgerald introduces these figures to suggest not only Gatsby's natural enemies but also his own.

Edward Tilyou inherited from his famous father, George C. Tilyou, the best-known "amusement" of its time, Steeplechase Park in Coney Island. In 1914, he was able to manage Steeplechase on the continued assumption that people wanted pleasant, moral, and innocent excitement, which Coney Island had given them since the turn of century. But by the early twenties such entertainment was no longer possible. Tilyou wrote in July 1922 (at the time the events of *The Great Gatsby* take place) that he now had to take into account a massive change in national character. He regarded it as a shift in cultural metabolism: "amusement" was now a matter of sensation and stimulation. Tilyou told his public why his business had to change its objectives and tactics: "You respond instantly to incandescent cupolas, the blare of music, the slam of scenic railways, the beating of tom-toms; and we give you what you want. . . . The tenseness of modern industry and business competition has keyed your nervous organism to such a pitch that you seek a sharp stimulus."[6] Tilyou, who was in the business of selling emotional satisfaction, understood that there was a new meaning to the idea of "nervous" Americans—who sound inordinately like the guests at Gatsby's second party.

I will be saying more about contemporary ideas of nervous energy, anxiety, and their moral effects; at this point I note only that Fitzgerald rewrote some truisms. In stories like " 'The Sensible Thing' " as well as in *The Great Gatsby* he addressed the differences between a heightened state of emotion and the moral weakness of mere nervousness, both notably experienced by Daisy Buchanan. The crowd at Gatsby's, as it might be perceived by a rather higher source, George Santayana, shows the new character of Americanism. Writing at exactly the same time, just before the events of the novel are said to have taken place, Santayana described "nervous depression" as "one of the most significant things in America." It was, he said, the sum of empty lives, especially of "forced optimism, routine, essential solitude."[7] There will be a good many examples of this particular set of meanings in the later part of Fitzgerald's story.

Tilyou understands that nervousness is now a quality that needs to be soothed and may be induced. James had hoped that nervous energy would be a natural reservoir for moral action. He knew that it was hard to define: "The terms have to remain vague; for though every man of woman born knows what is meant by such phrases as having a good vital tone, a high tide of spirits, an elastic temper, as living energetically, working easily, deciding firmly, and the like, we should all be put to our trumps if asked to explain in terms of scientific psychology just what such expressions mean."[8] *This* form of mental-moral energy was the source of a good American life. But Santayana was notably unsympathetic about James's argument. He wrote (1920) of James's essay, "Perhaps, like a democratic government, the soul is at its best when it merely collects and co-ordinates the impulses coming from the senses. The inner man is at times a tyrant, parasitical, wasteful, and voluptuous. At other times he is fanatical and mad."[9] "Great men" especially are outside the boundaries of what he identified as liberal Protestant optimism. And yet those boundaries are, to a certain extent, those of Fitzgerald's fiction.

Fitzgerald wants to believe the liberal Protestant conviction that the self can be remade. In a sense, both Nick and Gatsby have conventional faith in the efficacy of acts, hence in the innocence of motives. God is invisible in this novel not because of the issue of his existence but because human decision determines human fate. But as a critic of T. S. Eliot has pointed out, rationalist optimism could not stand up to the modernist mind.[10] Liberal Protestant hopefulness, with which both Nick's and Gatsby's narratives begin, is displaced by moral realism and the tragic sense of life. Liberal Protestant moral activism, however, had to be retained—as, indeed, it functioned in Fitzgerald's own intensely goal-oriented (and still partly Catholic) life.

For example, on the issue of giving in to "nerves," the liberal Protestant position stands firm in the text. I note that in the marketplace, Irving Babbitt's *Rousseau and Romanticism* (1919) had argued the case against "emotional indulgence" and for "moral strenuousness" in literature.[11] These rubrics apply to Fitzgerald's work in general and especially to *Gatsby,* whose protagonist is fabulously self-disinterested. More important, the standards brought to bear on his story by Nick Carraway are the standards of restraint defined by James at the turn of century and reasserted by Babbitt and others a generation later. There was a moral-literary terminology in use around 1920 of "always 'struggling forward' and never 'sinking back.' "[12] As the last pages of *The Great Gatsby* indicate, this language stayed in mind. As I hope to show, the character of "emotional indulgence" in *Gatsby,* especially in Daisy Buchanan, is a surrender to fate in the guise of nervous incapacity. But Nick sees his duty as the formulation of will by restraint with consequent moral action, not as the expression of subjective desire. He knows that desire and will have their imperatives—he respects those romantic imperatives on Gatsby's grand scale—but he is remorseless in his contempt for mere emotional self-interest. Self-interest exhausts the tolerance of a tolerant mind.

The sixth chapter of *The Great Gatsby* takes the liberal Protestant position. Gatsby's dreams proceed from innocence. We don't know quite how material or how

sexual they are—the language dims into romantic cir-
cumlocution—but they are the work not of the id but the
more abstract "imagination." Gatsby, like Nick Carraway,
has brakes on his desires and rejects the life of Dan Cody.
Some years later, when we see him at his first party, description is paradigm:

> I wondered if the fact that he was not drinking helped
> to set him off from his guests. . . . girls were putting
> their heads on men's shoulders in a puppyish, conviv-
> ial way, girls were swooning backward playfully into
> men's arms, even into groups knowing that someone
> would arrest their falls—but no one swooned back-
> ward on Gatsby and no French bob touched Gatsby's
> shoulder and no singing quartets were formed with
> Gatsby's head for one link. [41]

In what is essentially a tableau, Fitzgerald allegorizes
Wine, Women, and Song. I've briefly noted the Shavian
heroes who in the first quarter of the century, from
Caesar to Saint Joan, displayed both energy and innate
rectitude. They too are figures of moral, mental, and sexual chastity, never understood by the crowd or mob that
always surrounds them. Such figures have a common
context in William James: "Some austerity and wintry
negativity, some roughness, danger, stringency, and effort, some 'no! no!' must be mixed in, to produce the
sense of an existence with character and texture and

power."[13] And indeed, everywhere in James's work, are allusions to such literary examples. Gatsby's character is nowhere more mysterious than in his self-limitation. An act of will as rigorous as anything we can comprehend appears to go with what seems to be a lapse (or is it an assertion?) of imagination.

The sixth chapter debates both nervous energy and restraint of nerves. It tells us that before joining Dan Cody, Gatsby led a sexual life of "overwhelming self-absorption" (77). He does away (without conflict) with the life of the senses. He does not imitate Dan Cody in the pleasures of "an infinite number of women" (78), and he lets liquor alone. It would have been more interesting if *Daisy* had a rival in this story, but given the theory of Gatsby, it would be impossible, even undesirable, for her to have one.

Dan Cody, who is indeed "voluptuous," is part of a group of turn-of-the-century figures in the text. Very little mercy is shown to any of them, because they are historically representative. They are the relics of "the Victorian era" who show in grim satirical detail the fall of its egotism. Fitzgerald has taken a postwar idea and made some modifications. Recent work on the aftermath of World War I by Samuel Hynes emphasizes the presence of a particular kind of villain in writings of the twenties: "Victorian Old Men [who] represented the power of the past over the present . . . [and] the stupidities and the follies of the Victorian past."[14] These figures ruled the prewar world and oversaw its catastrophe. While public anxiety in the early twenties was often focused on "the younger generation," Fitzgerald had on his mind also that Victorian generation. Some in this group are either ineffectual, like Mr. Carraway, or aware, like Wolfsheim, that their time is over. But there is a much more powerful emphasis: Cody is "physically robust but on the verge of soft-mindedness" (78), while Jordan's aunt brings into the story her twice-defined trait, senility. The self-transcending brewer who built Gatsby's castle is merely daft; Mr. Gatz, worn-out by failure, is at the end of another dismal and even depressing American life.

Cody has been given a rough but useful chronology: he was born about 1857, joined the copper rush after 1875, was sent to sea by his caretaker-mistress in 1902, met Gatsby in 1907, and died hard and mindless in 1912. He is not only of the "real" West but also of the real America, a fact of life irreducible to philosophy. Whatever "civilization" may be, the term used by Tom Buchanan in beginning our social dialogue, and whatever "community" may be, the term used throughout the beginning of the century to identify ideal society, Cody is an impassable barrier to their ideas. He is the real majority; he does what men would do if they could. Fitzgerald has a particular strategy in dealing with wealth here, in "The Rich Boy" and in "The Diamond As Big as the Ritz." He is not concerned with the idea that wealth corrupts: instead, he works with the idea that wealth reveals. It allows personality to display what it *is,* hence its terrifically bad style and solipsism. The possession of wealth means that the possessor does not have to change his desires. Fitzgerald's rich men and women want only to be themselves without interruption. Dan Cody's yacht is simply a movable bar and bed. But we have to sense something about desire—in this text it wants unconsciousness. And it is the strength of both liberal Protestantism and the residual Catholicism of Fitzgerald that they resist this. One might say that it is the work of his novel to show that resistance.

But Fitzgerald was not unoriginal, and he did not accept unqualifiedly the idea that energy was premoral. Such is not the case for Gatsby and certainly not for others in the story. The extraordinary amount of theorizing by James and others about natural energies is not checkmated here, but it is certainly checked. Natural energies and the prized human quality of "vitality" may express themselves first in sensation—but they may also express themselves last in the complete, uncritical loss of self. "Energy" may have no innate morality; and in fact, it may not have a *plot.* In the case of the majority we remain very much what we began because change is too difficult. The key phrase for Cody may be not "savage" but "empty."

Cody is not simply the sum of life "of the frontier brothel and saloon" (78). His picture is generational, and we learn from him what it means to help "build up the country" (131). He connects to James J. Hill, to Rockefeller, and to Nick's uncle, who exhibits the same hardness of face and mind. If the idea of the frontier is satirically qualified, so is that of the country and its building up. Gatsby, at the beginning of his conscious life, believes that "the rock of the world" (77) is founded on imagination—or, at least, Nick, whose phrase it is, holds this belief for him. But Cody is in the story to state something different, that his world is the real world, both in the novel and in American life. It is occasionally uplifted, and some of its "vitality" spills over into higher things, but it remains unchanged. Most of the characters in the novel agree with him implicitly and imitate him with less success.

The subject of Cody, because of the summary quality, is a useful introduction to the people at Gatsby's second party and especially to Tom Buchanan, who follows hard on the heels of Cody's departure from the text. Tom is Dan Cody in a minor key, disguised by social conscience. His own indifference is hidden in manner and speech. The moment of comedy that attends his meeting with Gatsby is preceded and framed by Cody's open brutality. But the meeting is contrived and slippery with "civilization." It modernizes the Cody episode—there are the same components, men, women, drinks, hospitality. But the mode has become comedy of manners. There is much pumping of hands and twittering of invitations and downing of drinks and earnest worries about social behavior. Above all, there is talk—the scene is all talk and not much consequence. Yet there is one consequence, and this too has its American echoes—there is "lots of room" at the table (80) but not for Gatsby.

Tom keeps reappearing throughout the chapter—he has four separate entrances, so that he is structurally a necessity. The first manages to express many exclusionary thoughts in a single burst of statement: "By God, I may be old-fashioned in my ideas but women run around too much these days to suit me. They meet all kinds of crazy fish" (81). We are expected to translate: Tom does not want Daisy to live as he does, and he goes to his "ideas" for protection. The most interesting phrases are "these days" and "all kinds" because they establish the real parameters of his argument. Tom is formidably opposed to the present moment. He worries not only about Daisy but about all women, not only about Gatsby but about the encounter with those not known to him. These worries define one of his "ideas," that of civilization. It is his standard of judgment and also his definition of his own character. But we have been warned by Santayana that "Civilization . . . , although we are wont to speak the word with a certain unction, is a thing whose value may be questioned."[15] From this point on Tom will reenter dialogue as well as narrative, and his "ideas" and their "value" will determine the course of events. The reader will be expected to judge judgments.

We might begin with the judgment, also by Santayana, defining the great American issue of class responsibility introduced by Tom Buchanan:

Social inertia . . . perpetuates all the classes, and even such shifts as occur at once re-establish artificial conditions for the next generation. As a rule, men's station determines their occupation without their gifts determining their station. Thus stifled ability in the lower orders, and apathy or pampered incapacity in the higher, unite to deprive society of its natural leaders.[16]

Tom is a figure in a script he imagines, which goes something like this: he is a descendant of wealth and great social responsibility. He has married rightly and has even educated himself in the mores of his class. He is conscientious, willing to undertake the protection of righteousness. But the role he fulfills goes something like this: although he has lived the life of "pampered incapacity" described by Santayana while dreaming of being one of society's "natural leaders," he defines his responsibility as keeping the "lower orders" down, where they deserve to be. Having become a watchdog instead of a knight on horseback, he brings to a close one drama of genteel idealism, that of the aristocrat with a social conscience. The real script of his life will come into play from this point on. His function will be to exclude, his energies will center on envy, his bravery will be displaced by prudential fear.

The second party at Gatsby's is about passivity and excess, which turn out to be the same thing. Drunk or sober, quiet or turbulent, those at Gatsby's including Tom

and Daisy show the quality that Santayana called "monot-
ony"[17] and William James called—in many forms—the
deadly tedium of activity.[18] James has a huge vocabulary
of tedium vitae and refers constantly to indifference, passivity, reflexiveness, and, above all, mere unconscious existence. He emphasizes that these aspects of the not-
fully-human life are in fact part of its activity: the
"vibration of small interests and excitements that form
the tissue of our ordinary consciousness."[19] At Gatsby's
second and more realistic party, excitement is an external
quality, derived from booze and from the surrender of the
self rather than from its assertion. There are indeed internal energies, but they are not to be deciphered readily:
"A massive and lethargic woman, who had been urging
Daisy to play golf with her at the local club tomorrow,
spoke up in Miss Baedeker's defence: "Oh she's all right
now. When she's had five or six cocktails she always starts
screaming like that. I tell her she ought to leave it alone"
(83). Beneath the surface of indifference, James reminds
us in "Is Life Worth Living?" is a chaos of unexplained
feelings—mostly depressive. James hated the varieties of
determinism and believed that such feelings had causes
and cures. Like Santayana, he relates their occurrence to
the meaninglessness of mere existence; Fitzgerald seems
to have that and somewhat more in mind. The aggressive
screams have to be held back—like the outburst that
Daisy has had to hold back until she gets drunk and lets
us know what *actually* is "on" her mind. What is on Miss

Baedeker's mind seems to be what is on Fitzgerald's mind: she fears death by water—which is to say, she fears awakening itself.

The argument is not entirely developed from *The Waste Land*. Throughout the text Fitzgerald has considered the tedium of life in the way that the idea was stated by James. His language is reiterative, almost shocking when we realize the cumulative effect of *Accidie:* Daisy moves "languidly" and is impersonal "in the absence of all desire" (13). The last phrase is intuitive but may also be definitive. Even her jokes about being and doing—she is "paralyzed with happiness" (11)—are refractive. Mrs. McKee is also "languid" and gives us the unforgettable image of being frozen into repose "a hundred and twenty-seven times" (26). Jordan is always "bored." The text focuses briefly on those who are "lethargic," on the heated atmosphere that is "stifling," on a crowd without "consciousness." And of the major figures, Daisy looks for "some force" (118) to shape her life, something outside her life, with the energy she does not want to possess. These figures are not "in harmony with the nature of things."[20] They are radically unemotional in Jamesian terms. "Let us go straight at our question," James says (Did Eliot remember that phrase?), away from "drift" (Fitzgerald did remember that phrase) and toward the beginning of all things, "passion."[21] From this we are led to self-consciousness and to the most important thing of all, action on the basis of belief.[22] Gatsby is increasingly depicted by Fitzgerald as if he had a religious rather than a merely secular vision, and the Jamesian philosophy necessarily moves toward that end. Fitzgerald takes seriously some aspects of the liberal Protestant tradition: James ends this particular essay with the reminder that we are going to be wrong no matter how we act. But some ways of being wrong are better than others.

7

Belief and Will

At a distance of seventy years, and given the trend of the century's thought, it must now appear that Gatsby's idealism is a failure of reasonableness. Critics have defined that failure, assuming that Gatsby's love is either a "folly" or "illusion"[1] or, more pointedly, a "misdirected search for transcendence."[2] Gatsby is an unrealist, an immature romantic, childish, and even paranoid.[3] Even when we are sympathetic to Gatsby, we tend to think that he has not only mistaken the object of his quest but misconceived the idea of the quest. He seems to have parodied spirituality. But it may be that Gatsby is less heterodox and more representative of particular values of the early twentieth century. It was possible to believe, from the end of the Gilded Age until the Great War, that romantic idealism was both inevitable and morally healthy. Public Philosophy took seriously literature that stated love's idolatry, and it found a connection between different kinds of worship.

In 1912 Josiah Royce published his *Sources of Religious Insight,* a book from which was later excerpted a well-known commentary on William James and the idea of romantic love. Like James, Royce was fascinated by the contact between daily life and ideas and by the way it was expressed both in literature and philosophy. He, like James, regarded literature as another set of proofs for the demonstration of human nature.[4] In his essay "Individual Experience and Social Experience," Royce began to consider, through the texts of Coleridge, Dostoevsky, Shakespeare, and the Brownings, the problem of secular love as it becomes a form of religious love.[5] Royce was not opposed to the literary idea that secular love thinks of itself as religious love and has its own "unutterable visions":

> The religion of friendship and of love is a familiar human experience. James, in his fear of debasing religion by romantic or by grosser associations, unjustly neglects it in his study of "varieties." In fact, to seem to find the divine in the person of your idealised friend or beloved is a perfectly normal way of beginning your acquaintance with the means of grace. You meet, you love, and—you seem to be finding God. . . . There is no love so simple-minded that, if it be true love, the way of salvation may not seem to be opened through it to the lover.[6]

He was perfectly willing to accept that what "lovers dream" is what "religions tell." In that he represented the domestication of romantic ideas. Fitzgerald was famously influenced by Keats; but as much as the text of Keats mattered, recollections of idealism in his own time also mattered greatly. Throughout Fitzgerald's early life, romanticism had in certain ways become absorbed into moral discourse.

Romantic (and especially romantic Victorian) ideas were, however, heavily modified. Royce acknowledges the origin of some of his ideas in "Sonnets from the Portuguese" (among the lyrics he cites is "How do I love thee?" with the response, "I love thee with a love I seemed to lose / With my lost saints"). He understands the likelihood, in the modern moment, that religious feeling will become secular feeling; but he thinks of reversing the flow. Secular love may give rise to something more important: "Social experience seems to lie on the way to salvation."[7] He is self-censoring, but the subject includes sexual love. Living in a still identifiably Christian culture, Royce openly described his preoccupation, the process of becoming Christian. It was, Royce thought, *normative* for a man to begin with particular experiences, to sense divinity in a human object or cause, then to convert his understanding into religious affirmation. Both James and Royce are interested in the modes and in the stages of belief; and it would seem that Gatsby is at an early stage of imagination. The issue is not, I think, that Gatsby has mistakenly identified Daisy with his idea and his idea with religion. In doing what he has done he has recapitulated what most men are likely to do—and should do. Both Royce and James state that the loss of self in love, although expressed best in poetry, happens also to those without a language of feeling. They are much concerned with the uneducated mind.

Gatsby's persistence is generally regarded as the height of unrealism. But that is because his view of Daisy and of the past is unrealistic—it has nothing to do with the nature of his persistence. Toward the end of *The Philosophy of Loyalty,* Royce concludes that nearly all of our causes are lost causes. It is, he says, universal that we should devote ourselves to ideas that cannot be objectified. In fact: "every cause worthy . . . of lifelong service . . . shows sooner or later that it is a cause *which we cannot successfully express in any set of human experiences of transient joys and of crumbling successes.*"[8] In this "poor world of human sense-experience" we will never find an object worthy of our desires. Viewed in this way, Daisy and Gatsby are both paradigmatic. She is in some ways a moral failure—but she is also simply human nature in its actual form. From the beginning she could never answer to Gatsby's demands even if she were better. As for Gatsby, he is true to poetic sources of imagination that teach us first to love things human as if they were things spiritual.

The ending of James's *Pragmatism* begins with literature. At great length James cites Whitman, in order to demonstrate the redemptive possibilities of failure. He states that "loyalty" to "love" and even the loss of self in love allows us to reach what beatitude we can. James respects this deeply and does not at all find fault with the imagination that loses itself in the other. But again, like Royce, he envisions this as a stage in mental development: about as good as we are going to get in our unconsidered daily lives. And he adds something that turns this development into a drama—I have used the word "plot" in talking about James, and he is always conscious of the conception—"Identify your life therewith; then, through anger, losses, ignorance, ennui, whatever you thus make yourself, whatever you thus most deeply are, picks its way."[9] Fitzgerald seems to have taken half of this, as he has taken half of Royce, precisely because of the ironies that develop from the imitation of religious love. Gatsby's assertion of his own identity will lead no further because there are no longer Jamesian possibilities in his world. However, Nick Carraway understands two things: that there should be such possibilities and that few of us will acknowledge the necessity.

It had been possible, in the world of Fitzgerald's education, to be taught that we did in fact have a "ghostly heart," that one purpose of our existence was to serve "passion," and that love might be an "incarnation" of something much higher than ourselves. These are his words, words that he has chosen to retain in the text of this novel. There was no reason to doubt, Royce said, "at least a latent belief in the superhuman reality" of your cause.[10] Gatsby has many flaws, but they do not include the conception of sacred love. What is "too much" to be demanded? Not the idea that Daisy is worth devotion nor the idea that life changes profoundly, in its very identity, through love.

Walter Lippmann stated in 1914 that it was typically American to confuse the happy past with the happy future. He thought a majority of Americans did so: "we persist in recalling what is by its very nature irrevocable."[11] He added that "the American temperament" proceeded from "the warmth of memory"—and that it "leans generally to a kind of mystical anarchism" centered on the person.[12] That is to say, American ideals become embodied in human character rather than in abstractions about the state. At the end of the twenties he returned to the argument about the energies of the past: "The memory of an age of innocence has haunted the whole of mankind. It has been a light behind their present experience which cast shadows upon it, and made it seem insubstantial and not inevitable. Before this life, there had been another which was happier. And so they reasoned that what once was possible must somehow be possible again." Lippmann believed that the search for past happiness recapitulated itself in American lives and became absorbed into our national imagination: "as an intimation of our own inward experience, and like an uneasy spirit it intrudes itself upon our most realistic efforts to accept the world as we find it. . . . It is a deep conviction that happiness is possible."[13] The idea of recapturing the past—regaining Paradise—was necessarily part of American social expectation and, he thought, politically important for the shaping of our future. Gatsby's imagination and his desires seem more definable and much less exotic. Lippmann concludes, regretfully and in the Jamesian vein, that we can have only limited forms of happiness—but in order to get even those we have first to understand that our "memory" of innocent desire underlies all possibility.

The narrative, so full of reminders of a lost moment, of a distant Eden, of past memories, constitutes a frame for Gatsby's own unmediated and absolutist vision of past happiness. But he is at a stage of idealism, not of egotism.

The endings of chapters 5 and 6 go back to ideas that are themselves "uncommunicable forever." We have heard them, Fitzgerald writes, "a long time ago." They are now barely at the level of consciousness. He is referring to Daisy's "incarnation" and to the quasi-religious act of Gatsby's imagination. The language of religion lingers in Fitzgerald's text and for a reason (87). We are always confusing things, Royce wrote—the "plain man" especially being liable to find God in some "vision" of earth, through his own "private will."[14] But we are helpless, Royce added, "to turn the vision into a practical reality," an idea that I take to be the upshot of Fitzgerald's seventh chapter.

We are back to secular earth in this chapter. In fact, we begin again at the beginning, with Nick entering the Buchanan house to find the telephone ringing and Daisy and Jordan reclining on the couch "like silver idols" (90). Clearly the duplication of setting, action, and tone is meant to indicate stasis. Life is in suspension, consciousness at the usual material level. Tom talks about money; Daisy and Jordan are beautifully immobile in another tableau of complete self-containment. But conversation becomes strangely transcendent, and even apocalyptical, before it turns again to those American issues with which the novel began.

In his unconscious way Tom reminds all with him of vanishing possibilities: there may not be a promised end in his imagination; nevertheless, someday "the earth's going to fall into the sun" (92). He invites Nick and Gatsby to see his "place," but what becomes visible is a place beyond places, "the scalloped ocean and the abounding blessed isles" (92), a contradiction to the imagination of things as they are. Daisy is far more conscious than Tom—she knows that there are only "the next thirty years" (92), and that something meaningful has to be done with them. (She echoes Myrtle, who knows that you can't live forever. However, Myrtle makes her decisions on that knowledge.) After thirty years, an almost Platonic number in the text, the earth may as well have fallen into the sun. Jordan is pragmatic, arguing that life is a series of beginnings each year—but she too sees no "end." The dialogue matters not only because Daisy admits that she loves Gatsby but because she admits that she knows what love is supposed to do, give meaning to short life. When she asks, "What'll we do with ourselves?" (92), it becomes clear that she understands all the issues: that she too knows about the necessity of becoming (although, as she phrases the issue, it looks as if she plans on its consistent, daily evasion). At best, she is on the verge of a great, really a heroic acknowledgment, and Tom realizes this when he recognizes her "as someone he knew a long time ago" (93). Daisy has made a tremendous effort to awaken. This chapter affects us not only because Gatsby's dream fails but because Daisy comes so close to awakening from the dream of her life.

This chapter especially brings to bear a sense of the permanent and transcendent against the earthly. It makes a great many references to life and death, and Heaven and Hell, and time and space. Like the Porter in *Macbeth,* the conductor on the train lets us know where we may well be: "Hot! . . . Hot! . . . Hot! . . . Is it hot enough for you? Is it hot? Is it . . . ?" It is hot enough so that, reductively, no man need care "whose flushed lips he kissed, whose head made damp the pajama pocket over his heart" (89). The "common store of life" (90) is depicted, exhausted, and we are invited to think of the limits of will and imagination, we are even forgiven for having done so.

Paralyzed with the heat, Daisy dreams of coldness, tells Gatsby that he always looks so cool—even, in a replay of her wedding night, wants to reenact a "cold bath" in a hotel. The heat is palpable, the signature of earthly limits. Only in the fall, when the cold comes, can life start "all over again" (92). There are many resonances: "One autumn night, five years before" (86), when the leaves were falling, life did change with the change of the year. But they are in the element now, and the heat makes things that much more real, defined, and unchangeable. As Jordan says, "Imagine marrying anybody in this heat!" (99). The line is addressed to the reader.

The context is civilized paralysis, as described, often, by the Public Philosophy. The text plays variations on the idea of entropy: Jordan and Daisy "can't move" (90); George Wilson is "run down" and "sick" (95–96), a silent totem sitting by the road and staring at movement; even the sun is losing its energy; the magnificent Plaza Hotel is "stifling" (98); Gatsby's dream is "dead" (105); and he and Daisy leave the scene "isolated like ghosts even from our pity" (105). Jordan has it precisely right, and in the Jamesian vein: life without the consciousness of renewal is "morbid" (92).

This chapter completes what the first chapter begins. The dialogue continues about house and home and wife and family and the "institutions" that make up civilized life. In some central way the text needs to address these things and to do it through the imagination of the adversary Tom Buchanan. One of the great things about Tom Buchanan's mental life is that he lies transparently—but although no one believes him, people accept what he has to say. Jordan and Daisy have agreed at the beginning of the story that a sound family life is good for the soul; Daisy will eventually agree—accept—that when Tom goes off on a spree he really loves her in his heart. It matters greatly that all should agree on the truth of things transparently false. In the Dantean circumstances of this chapter, there will be great refusals of the mind. Fitzgerald is interested in the rationalizing of act and decision, which is why Tom Buchanan is superabundantly equipped in this text with the "theoretical" language of "ideas."

Tom is as inventive about life in general as he is about it in particular. But it will be Tom's idea of "civilization" that prevails:

> "Self control!" repeated Tom incredulously. "I suppose the latest thing is to sit back and let Mr. Nobody from Nowhere make love to your wife. Well, if that's the idea you can count me out. . . . Nowadays people begin by sneering at family life and family institutions and next they'll throw everything overboard and have intermarriage between black and white."
>
> Flushed with his impassioned gibberish he saw himself standing alone on the last barrier of civilization. [101]

It is the imitation of a sacred rage. But although Tom is debating sex he seems not to be sexually aware. Gatsby is "Mr. Nobody" and Daisy is generically "your wife." Both of them lack physical shape or desires. In the first chapter Tom has been identified with "opinion" and "idea"; in the sixth chapter, once more with "ideas" (which are "old-fashioned"); and here, in the seventh chapter, with a final "idea" of something outside himself that makes him what he is. He is very good at the imitation of action—being counted "out" suggests that an initiative has been taken, a vote recorded. How wrong is he? Not very: his house will again become A Doll's House; Daisy will relinquish sexual love for "family institutions"; and neither Jordan nor Daisy will challenge his views on "the modern world." If his "ideas" about any and all things are so transparently empty, so unconvincing and stupid, how do they win?

As Tom puts the matter, relying on his signature phrase, "sometimes she gets foolish ideas in her head and doesn't know what she's doing" (102). There are wheels within wheels: he is right about Daisy, has confused ideas with feelings, doesn't realize that what he has just said is fully self-descriptive. In order for him to win Daisy back he has to do very little, simply give her some interior lines on which to withdraw. Nick says that Daisy finally loses both intentions and courage—but the equivalent of those two "ideas" is will and feeling. Tom knows that it is much easier to live without those things, and what he offers

Daisy is not love renewed but the infinitely greater attractions of emotions unfelt, of invulnerability to them. As a moment of decision arrives, Daisy becomes morally conscious, and "her eyes fell on Jordan and me with a sort of appeal, as though she realized at last what she was doing" (103). She almost makes it across the line but later withdraws "further and further into herself" (105). James states in the beginning of *Pragmatism* that reality is "tangled, muddy, painful and perplexed." We do things not from motives of evil but because we want to keep out "of all definite touch with concrete facts and joys and sorrows."[15] One of the privileges of wealth, as Fitzgerald depicts it, is that it allows this privileged unconsciousness.

The three last chapters of this novel have to do a lot of work. They are packed with episodes, and the long chapter 7 contains most of the action of the book. The deadly heat, a figure for unconsciousness ("where the sun beats, / And the dead tree gives no shelter")[16] drives even Nick to the "limits" of sympathy:

It was seven o'clock when we got into the coupé with him and started for Long Island. Tom talked incessantly, exulting and laughing, but his voice was as remote from Jordan and me as the foreign clamor on the sidewalk or the tumult of the elevated overhead. Human sympathy has its limits and we were content to let all other tragic arguments fade with the city lights behind. Thirty—the promise of a decade of loneliness, a thinning list of single men to know, a thinning brief-case of enthusiasm, thinning hair. But there was Jordan beside me who, unlike Daisy, was too wise ever to carry well-forgotten dreams from age to age. As we passed over the dark bridge her wan face fell lazily against my coat's shoulder and the formidable stroke of thirty died away with the reassuring pressure of her hand.

So we drove on toward death through the cooling twilight. [106]

The passage sums up those other passages in the text that challenge intelligibility and resist any impulse to order what we are doing and thinking. The narration emphatically and strategically converts itself to what James called the "chaos of experience." We cannot hear or think or perceive, and we certainly cannot act. There is no chance to *apply* our values, and in a kind of fog or paralysis, we withdraw not only from decision but from consciousness. But, James said, if the nature of things is resistant it nevertheless remains our intellectual and moral duty to "wrest order out of the swirl."[17] Tom is simply insentient, Jordan resists consciousness, and Nick finds himself in the dilemma of awareness-inaction. These things had long been considered by Fitzgerald. The individual is constituted ("The Offshore Pirate," 1920) by the play of consciousness that takes the active form of courage: "And courage to me meant ploughing through that dull gray mist that comes down on life—not only overriding people and circumstances but overriding the bleakness of things. A sort of insistence on the value of life and the worth of transient things."[18] The values—and the figure of forcing order out of fog—have become embedded in Fitzgerald's mind. Ardita in this story argues for ever more clarity of will and purpose and for the consequent return of our early "joy" and "hope" and "spontaneity."

Nothing of Tom's "incessant" talk is recollected or even understood, but it cannot really be ignored. It is in its turn framed by the New York "clamor" and "tumult of the elevated overhead" that drowns out one's own reactive capability. The prose is enormously skillful, projecting chaotic sound as vacant idea. There is now very little sense of that "insistence" on the value of life and the recognition of essences. Our own individualism has been compromised as we watched while Nick was drained of his moral energies, forced to admit that he is at the end of his human sympathies, passively "content" only not to know or hear. Nick understands that he has in some way compromised his own "enthusiasm," which is more than it sounds, a virtue of the age he has left behind. The age of Roosevelt and William James had matched "vitality" to its manifested form of "vigor" and regarded "enthusiasm" as a necessary ground for belief. "Thirty" is more than a number in the text; both Nick and Daisy consider it first the sign of meaningless life and then of death. Jordan's wan presence promises forgetfulness and even comfort, which may be desirable but are not values.

The long, drawn-out account of Gatsby's defeat ends in indecision. Myrtle Wilson's death, which occurs almost immediately, is caused by decisiveness. Her "tremendous vitality" (107) is much more than sexual: without thinking things through, she does what she wants to do. Myrtle gets one last speech twelve words long. It is very much in character: four pronouns dominate those twelve words, and three of them, definitively, are "me." Myrtle imagines a self in every clause and, dramatically imperative, invites an audience to witness this scene from her life: "Beat me! . . . Throw me down and beat me, you dirty little coward!" (107). She sees herself on silent film. The first description of her death (there are a number of replays, each with more information to add) is character in action: the car "wavered tragically for a moment and then disappeared around the next bend" (107). Myrtle, characteristically, cuts straight across the road while Daisy, characteristically, moves hesitantly in curved lines.

Gatsby's heroism is self-effacing: only three other people will know about it, and only one of them will care. To say that it is also in character is to choose a kind of character to be stated. Gatsby may well be innately brave, and saving Daisy may be the equivalent of unconsidered wartime cold-bloodedness. But firmness of mind becomes heroism only when he decides to take the blame.

Fitzgerald has a powerful grasp of the issues; he concentrates on the aftermath because sensibility is then displaced by decision, when something we have to call moral happens. Until now Nick has admired Gatsby's imagination, but there has been a turn in the story: from here on, characters divide themselves into adversary groups.

But there is something more important than bravery-heroism and more important even than the conscious choice of a difficult option. Throughout the seventh chapter it has been a deep temptation to escape facts and submerge intentions, to abandon what William James called the "will," or volition that makes action possible. The dialogue has been almost Spenserian, full of allegorical clamor and chaos and cognitive dissonance and confusion and perceptual doubt. Passage after passage registers the refusal of consciousness and intention. Daisy especially is "nervous" or incapacitated, both at the Plaza, then at the scene of Myrtle Wilson's death in the valley of ashes. Fitzgerald has gone to great lengths to show nearly all of his major characters in this chapter in a particular way, confused within a larger confusion. The issue is not only that they make immoral decisions but that they retreat into themselves (Nick will be a memorable exception) rather than cope with the incoherence around them.

This is a very particular way of looking at things. The text addresses contextual ideas that force particular interpretations of attitudes and acts. It deals with the nature of reality as it is perceived by the mind and by the refusal of the mind to engage it. It describes in tremendous detail the retreat of the human mind not only from consciousness but especially from *relationship*. The Jamesian idea of "effort" has been given up, and the mind voluntarily lapses into "spontaneous drift." Daisy is "very nervous" and without command of herself. She has to make several decisions, the first of which is clearly understandable. But her second decision—equally understandable—is more culpable. A very clear framework had been provided for the evaluation of act and intention: we see it defined by James as "the 'reasonable type' of decision." Such a decision can be made only if the mind asserts the values of consciousness and rejects the powers of circumstance. Why is Daisy so darkened by what is clearly an accident? Because it is less than human, according to James ("we shy away like frightened horses"), to refuse to resist: "I have put the thing in this ultra-simple way because I want more than anything else to emphasize the fact that volition is primarily a relation, not between our Self and extra-mental matter (as many philosophers still maintain), but between our Self and our own states of mind."[19]

Fitzgerald reflects more than the ethics and psychology of William James. He is describing the mainstream of ethical and psychological thought and also his own allegiance to it. For example, Janet Oppenheim's superb account of the heavily moralized diagnosis of anxiety in the nineteenth century ends with a review of beliefs from the turn of century to the early twenties. She points out that "nervous" disorders were rarely judged on purely medical grounds: the advent of World War I and its incidence of shell shock only confirmed the theory that "the doctor had to compel 'the patient to pull himself together and to resume control over himself.' "[20] It was essential to exercise "self-restraint" over anxiety and to assert the "moral sense" rather than give in to depression. " 'The Sensible Thing,' " which is embedded in *The Great Gatsby,* goes into voluminous detail on the guilt attached to being "nervous." In fact, we get a useful definition of female nervous indulgence: George O'Kelly "knew what 'nervous' meant—that she was emotionally depressed, that the prospect of marrying into a life of poverty and struggle was putting too much strain upon her love."[21] As for male neurosis, the reiterative use of "nervous" to describe himself means weak, self-pitying, and untrustworthy.[22] "Enervation" and confusion were widely perceived as moral failures.[23]

Daisy's response to Myrtle Wilson's death takes the form of a Jamesian fall out of human identity. Fitzgerald makes it plain that the real issues are those of the denial of human relationship and the assertion of the mere unmediated self. The accident is just that, something unpreventable; but the response is a moral revelation. Clearly, we have natural sympathies for both Myrtle and

Daisy. But Fitzgerald's strategy is to remove our sympathy from Daisy and to begin at this point to clarify issues under a very harsh light. Here is William James on the boundaries of the virtue of tolerance:

> When a dreadful object is presented, or when life as a whole turns up its dark abysses to our view, then the worthless ones among us lose their hold on the situation altogether, and either escape from its difficulties by averting their attention, or if they cannot do that, collapse into yielding masses of plaintiveness and fear. The effort required for facing and consenting to such objects is beyond their power to make.[24]

To be modern is to wish to deny either that anyone is worthless or that fear is contemptible. But Fitzgerald has made it impossible now "to reserve all judgments" (5). We are past that point. And we are firmly within a traditional moral universe that has strict demarcations. Part of the intense moral conflict in Fitzgerald's work is that between past and present, between new selves and still resonant ideas.

8

Ruins and Order

*T*he *Great Gatsby* contains some of the most familiar landscape in American literature, very little of it natural. It describes places urban and man-made, although to get from one to another of them the text traverses an idea of nature. Flowers and shrubs are yellow or green; water and sky are appropriate blue spaces. We see the great bridge but not the water it goes over. There is almost no perspective, and Fitzgerald does not establish relationships between natural objects. We do not know where Gatsby's jonquils or hawthorn are, or more than the general location of his gardens.[1] They are themselves part of the backdrop, the subject being understood as human disposition and act.

One of the most telling ways in which *The Great Gatsby* differentiates itself is its view of nature as context without connection. Nature as system has no relationship

to human activity except, occasionally, to make it difficult. Nature as presence seems not to motivate any single
character—the aesthetic responses of Nick Carraway are
impelled by line, color, and light. Fitzgerald is content to
leave Tom Buchanan's active sexuality as the product of
boredom and opportunity, while Daisy's passive sexuality
lies unlocated between determinism and choice. The
story is told as a sequence of human intentions and consequences traversing time and space, much like a political history of the United States. Nature is tremendously
present—but as symbol and myth. The entire foreground
is man and his acts and his works. That is one reason why
their disappearance affects us. They are all that is, and
when they leave the stage it is empty, even the vast con-
tinent at the end.

Virtually all activity in the narrative occurs within or
beside places that embody ideas: the Buchanan colonial
mansion, Myrtle's showcase apartment, and especially
Gatsby's *Joyeuse Garde*. The barest allusions work to dis-
integrate natural specificities and to specify human design: "My house looks well, doesn't it?" he demanded.
"See how the whole front of it catches the light" (70). It
is a more complicated statement than we might expect
from Gatsby, suggesting in many ways desire for the mastery of not only form but circumstance. Gatsby understands that property is character—but Nick understands
that the relationship of self to nature is that of windows

to light. The clause about "front" or surface is unconsciously revelatory.

Tocqueville wrote that democracies were vulnerable, beginning in individualism, a social virtue, but ending in egotism, "which leads a man to think of all things in terms of himself." About prosperity, Tocqueville was doubtful: he thought that "houses" and "acres" were liable to become altogether too metaphysical for Americans; "the soul cleaves to them; it dwells on them every day and in great detail; in the end they shut out the rest of the world and sometimes come between the soul and God."[2] He thought that this feeling about property was natural, inevitable, and that it was exaggerated by wealth, which "enervated" our minds. What else could be worshiped in a democracy, so empty of the past, but the works of the self? It was characteristically democratic to have such deeply secularized feelings about property and to believe that success represented more than success. Gatsby is a figure in an American drama specifically contemporary and also much older than the decade of the twenties.

We keep going through Gatsby's house with Owl Eyes, with Daisy, with Gatsby, with Mr. Gatz, alone with Nick—this progress is one of the repeated rhythms of the text. I can't overemphasize the powers of repetition: this is a book full of doublets and triplets, with key words insistently repeated, with a story that itself seeks to be retold. A substantial proportion of the text is devoted to each of the excursions through Gatsby's place. Each time we go through it we learn more about it, feel its symbolic weight. The second chapter, at Myrtle Wilson's, describes a false Versailles, but in the next chapter Gatsby's place has the styled immensity that is so much admired by Myrtle and by the magazines that have given her ambitions, has the order of a great household dependent on many hands. In the fifth chapter, when Daisy arrives, we too are overwhelmed by silk and gold. It is a completed world and, given American conceptions, is not missing anything.

The eighth chapter begins with a powerful description of this house and the last chapter ends with one. These chapters describe it in different ways. Mr. Gatz sees it from the outside while he is inside:

> His pride in his son and in his son's possessions was continually increasing and now he had something to show me.
>
> "Jimmy sent me this picture." He took out his wallet with trembling fingers. "Look there."
>
> It was a photograph of the house, cracked in the corners and dirty with many hands. He pointed out every detail to me eagerly. "Look there!" and then sought admiration from my eyes. He had shown it so often that I think it was more real to him now than the house itself. [134]

Gatsby in turn invites Daisy's response to his "possessions." But Tom Buchanan is no less proprietary. In the
opening chapter he tells Nick, "I've got a nice place here"
(10) and then displays it—restlessly—in very much the
way that Gatsby later shows his place. He too is associated with windows reflecting and capturing natural light,
with the design of a setting for which Nature is simply a
source of protons. Like Mr. Gatz, they both think of the
act of witnessing their places as a culmination. Display is
definitely one of Tom's "ideas"—he repeats himself when
talking to Gatsby in the seventh chapter: "I'd like you to
have a look at the place" (92). Everyone involved knows
that to "look" at place and possession is to see character
and idea. The owners may insist, but the witnesses com-
ply. Nick is in no way more completely American than in
his willingness to allow his interlocutors to believe that
he sees the world with the same sense of measure that
they do.

When we enter Gatsby's place we see something that
Mr. Gatz passes over. He dwells on size and shape and on
"height and splendor"; Nick and the reader will concen-
trate on the style of interior and furnishings. The text describes the house variously as castle, court, tower, library—the sum of all of which is, I think, a museum.
Tom Buchanan has been complaining of American ne-
glect of the arts and of "civilization" but Gatsby has been
doing his part: his place goes back over the centuries as

far as Gothic England and retraces (purchased) world
history in a dimly chronological way. Everything in it
adds up to America in 1922. History has been reconsti-
tuted, as in the rooms of Hearst's castle, San Simeon. To
look at either place is to see objectified proof that the past
has been incorporated in the present, that it has become
a possession also. Design imitates history, or the scrambled American notion of it, an idea that explains something about the chronology of Gatsby's interiors. But the
periods have become America.

Addison Mizner, the extraordinary architect and public relations man who was responsible for much of the
"period craze" noted by Nick, had sound commercial reasons for wanting "his buildings to look old."[3] Mizner's cli-
ents were "new owners" who needed instant ancestry.
The Mizner style sounds like satire: designs "based on
Romanesque ruins that had been rebuilt by the trium-
phant Saracens, added to by a variety of conquerors
bringing in new styles from the Gothic to the Baroque,
and picturesquely cracked up by everything from batter-
ing rams to artillery duels between Wellington and
Napoleon's marshals."[4] It is no wonder that Gatsby's place
has a "postern" and a "feudal silhouette" for sorties and
defense. A Mizner house was a product that might (in
Nick Carraway's conscious terminology) suggest "home,"
"family," "clan," "tradition," and, especially, "ancestors."
Gatsby knows that that last phrase matters. Personal
identity requires legitimation by history, something that

he has thought about. He wants not wealth or interior decoration but that his identity be confirmed, turned into generations of biography.

Fitzgerald added something to the "period craze" for age and ruin, taking the ideas seriously. If they had become American ideas, then they had to be understood as such. He is very much interested in the way that "wealth" becomes "acres," and he takes pains to describe how the Buchanans got their house and how they left it, what happens to Gatsby's place, and, throughout the text, the myriad events and transitions in rented rooms, suites, and apartments. He gives the provenance of possessions and emphasizes their significance in biographical and historical terms.

He does so, however, in a deconstructive way. In the "Scenes and Situations" part of his notebooks, Fitzgerald later describes an unnamed couple driving along the main street of a town on the Mississippi. They are looking for something meaningful in which to locate themselves. But the buildings that flash past are impermanence objectified, a scrambled chronology that shifts from medieval Flemish to Corinthian to Petit Trianon to those final relics of the Victorian generation, gloomy brownstones and "dark frame horrors" and "grim red brick" row houses of "the late 90's." Imitative and faked design implies more than architecture: the description is another of Fitzgerald's many rejections of the nation's and his own recent past. The two see finally "new houses again, bright blinding flowery lawns. These swept by, faded past, enjoying their moment of grandeur; then waiting there in the moonlight to be outmoded as had the frame, cupolaed mansions of lower down and the brownstone piles of older Crest Avenue in their turn."[5] This is both history—discontinuous and useless to the present—and the flux of American identity. There is no sense of connection or obligation.

We don't really go anywhere in this story; everywhere comes to Gatsby's. Although Fitzgerald knew a great deal about the *Follies,* for example, we aren't given a scene on Broadway. Gatsby's house is a stage, and the *Follies,* jazz, dance, and even haute couture take their turns on it. Both past and present meet in this place, the myriad things from European centuries and those who now possess their meanings. When Fitzgerald later wrote about the jazz age and specified, "May one offer in exhibit the year 1922!" he emphasized that "we were the most powerful nation" in the world. But he had little interest in politics or applications of power and concluded that we had inherited the attitudes and *styles* of the past.[6] We either kept or rejected them, it being only a matter of choice. What was not bequeathed was bought. But the important thing was that the present had simply soaked up the past. The past is artifact.

Gatsby's house is full of all those things that make up America in 1922. It certainly contains the phenomenological possibilities: from a man quietly doing liver exercises on the floor in happy isolation, to the sanctum of a bedroom with lares and penates (at the hidden heart of it is a picture of Dan Cody), to the rowdy crowds of the American scene. Seeing the lights of his place, Gatsby reminds himself to go to Coney Island, and Nick says that it "looks like the world's fair" (64). In fact, it looks like America in the early twenties. And Gatsby is never more "a regular Belasco" (38) than when he connects the realities and illusions of the moment—for him the house is a working theater.

The house goes through many transformations. When first experienced it is full of rhythm, style, color, and movement: "already the halls and salons and verandas are gaudy with primary colors and hair shorn in strange new ways and shawls beyond the dreams of Castile" (34). It is the present historical moment in America, combining the absolute new with possession of the European past. Yet by the end of the night there remains only the moon, "surviving the laughter and the sound of his still glowing garden. A sudden emptiness seemed to flow now from the windows and the great doors" (46). The note will be repeated of styles—and what we take to be realities—disappearing into the silence of nature.

Fitzgerald devotes a considerable part of his text to the devolution of Gatsby's castle. In the beginning, what it contains seems strange but real. But the lights "go out" after the second party; and after Gatsby resumes with Daisy, "the whole caravansary had fallen in like a card house" (88). It becomes eventually a deserted space, corresponding in important ways to the perception, in the early twenties, of new American realities:

> His house had never seemed so enormous to me as it did that night when we hunted through the great rooms for cigarettes. We pushed aside curtains that were like pavilions and felt over innumerable feet of dark wall for electric light switches—once I tumbled with a sort of splash upon the keys of a ghostly piano. There was an inexplicable amount of dust everywhere and the rooms were musty as though they hadn't been aired for many days. I found the humidor on an unfamiliar table with two stale dry cigarettes inside. Throwing open the French windows of the drawing room we sat smoking out into the darkness. [115]

At the very end the house is tellingly described as if it were itself a text, as an "incoherent failure" (140) written into the shore. This part of the ending is plangent, full of the resonances of literary themes. There are as well some political themes.

Fitzgerald did not originate the idea of American ruins or its exemplification. Here is Tocqueville on another island in New York:

> The whole island was one of those delightful New World solitudes that almost make civilized man regret

the savage life. The marvels of a vigorous vegetation told of the incomparable wealth of the soil. The deep silence of the North American wilderness was only broken by the monotonous cooing of wood pigeons or the tapping of green woodpeckers on the trees' bark. Nature seemed completely left to herself, and it was far from my thoughts to suppose that the place had once been inhabited. But when I got to the middle of the island I suddenly thought I noticed traces of man. Then, looking closely at everything around, I was soon convinced that a European had come to seek a refuge in this place. But how greatly his work had changed appearance! The logs he had hastily cut to build a shelter had sprouted afresh; his fences had become live hedges, and his cabin had been turned into a grove. Among the bushes were a few stones blackened by fire around a little heap of ashes; no doubt that was his hearth, covered with the ruins of a fallen chimney. For some little time I silently contemplated the resources of nature and the feebleness of man; and when I did leave the enchanted spot, I kept saying sadly: "What! Ruins so soon!"[7]

The mood expressed goes far beyond Tocqueville, into early romanticism and past that to Enlightened melancholy. Beyond Gatsby's ruins are the ruins of Time. Fitzgerald surrounds his events with a penumbra, makes them into the current forms of everlasting truths. However, he was not the only author of the early part of the century to do so.

Tocqueville noted the "restless" passion and "immoderate desire" of American dreams.[8] We see these dreams in a contained form as the novel begins, but by the end they too have devolved, into nightmares. The last two chapters are sleepless, and their dreams go in reverse, from life "beginning over again" with universal meaning, to an ending in chaos: "I couldn't sleep all night; a fog-horn was groaning incessantly on the Sound, and I tossed half sick between grotesque reality and savage frightening dreams" (115). Fitzgerald repeats certain connections between dissonance, a dead landscape, empty or unintelligible houses, and water that drowns human traces. As I've noted, there are political implications.

Edith Wharton's tremendous assessment of American life before the Great War describes a lost social order and those who were "swept away with it."[9] Her Victorian New York, she wrote, would become "as much a vanished city as Atlantis or the lowest layer of Schliemann's Troy . . . swept to oblivion with the rest."[10] Like Fitzgerald, she resonates to social change, but she also understands that the new displaces the old without replacing it. The *figurae* of oblivion were much on writers' minds. For example, according to Walter Lippmann, "there have gone into dissolution not only the current orthodoxy, but the social order and the ways of living which supported it."[11] Edmund Wilson's notebooks for June 1922, when the story of *The Great Gatsby* begins, contain long and pointed passages, of which this is a sample, about vanished great houses on the unwilling shore:

> Swiss chalets bleached out like mussel shells, Italian villas with elephantiasis, turreted medieval castles like Maxfield Parrish worse debauched, giant mosques, English half-timbered manor houses swollen to a toneless hugeness . . . ready to capsize like sand castles. . . . All this must once have been thought attractive, have possessed the charms and the movements of life. . . . The sea has no leeway here to spread its crests in ease and recede . . . only so much sterile debris that might better be chivied away and rhythmically pulverized in the universal solvent of the waves.[12]

The location is New Jersey—as Wilson moves north on the eastern shore he makes his point quite plain: between land and sea are American houses that imply a "whole civilization."[13] Edith Wharton had mixed feelings about her Lost Atlantis, and Wilson was in a frame of mind, perhaps a political mood, to welcome the conception. In the March 15, 1922, issue of the *New Republic* (75–77) he had written from France about great good places and their meanings: "the yellow long-windowed chateaux sunk deep in the countryside" were "a part of the burden these people must always drag with them." It was good for them to be historically "abolished." And also in America: "what a flood might sweep off the dam! what a thundering torrent of energy" might destroy the structures of our past and present. Pound had summed up a botched civilization in terms of its wrecked art and artifacts; Eliot had written in "Gerontion" that his house and ours was "a decayed house"; and Yeats had begun to seek his own symbols of the good life from the parks and towers of the untouchable past. Fitzgerald's use of the figure of dissolution complicates Tocqueville's pathos, refers itself to the language of modern resentment over failed promise. "That huge incoherent failure" (140) is America itself, a great good place on the edge of floodtide. But Fitzgerald had, in some ways, a more alert mind than those who saw Atlantis in Niagara.

The narrative begins to complete itself with the reminder that the story it tells must contend with a manufactured public version:

> After two years I remember the rest of that day, and that night and the next day, only as an endless drill of police and photographers and newspaper men in and out of Gatsby's front door. . . . Someone with a positive manner, perhaps a detective, used the expression "mad man" as he bent over Wilson's body that afternoon, and the adventitious authority of his voice set the key for the newspaper reports next morning.

Most of those reports were a nightmare—grotesque, circumstantial, eager and untrue. When Michaelis's testimony at the inquest brought to light Wilson's suspicions of his wife I thought the whole tale would shortly be served up in racy pasquinade—but Catherine, who might have said anything, didn't say a word. . . . So Wilson was reduced to a man "deranged by grief" in order that the case might remain in its simplest form. And it rested there. [127]

And yet Gatsby's story *began* as an item of gossip and newspaper coverage of the Fuller-McGee case of 1922.[14] Edward M. Fuller, who was involved with Arnold Rothstein, was then indicted for brokerage fraud, something that Tom Buchanan worries about greatly at the Plaza. Fitzgerald refers back to his sources, feeling, evidently, that he must in some way acknowledge them but also demonstrate what they have missed and what has to be done to them. They have given us an essential national story without knowing what it means. He repeats the tactic of implying—in this case stating—an alternative story. Gatsby's story in the press—as "confused" as any "news" described by Walter Lippmann—would be all that remains without Fitzgerald's mediation, although the public might be just as happy with a lesser construction. The two stories coexist momentarily, inviting comparison. One version is associated with the seriousness of the novel, the other with the triviality not only of the press but of the great American audience.

Fitzgerald's argument with mass media is stated a number of times within the novel and in other works. It fits into a chronology. In 1920, H. L. Mencken had written in "American Culture" that the salient character of the American press was neither its dishonesty nor lack of dignity and honor: it was an "incurable fear of ideas."[15] He linked this to the role of the press as "mob-master." That is, the press served to *prevent* the explanation of experience because readers did not want to "scrutinize" problems, facts, or ideas—and the audience had to be kept happy, unreflective of real American issues. Walter Lippmann's thesis on the futility of the press appeared shortly thereafter in *Public Opinion* (1922), focusing on the untruth of what usually passed for "news." Fitzgerald's argument on the communication of truth depends on a prior argument by Lippmann. A "report" is inherently selective, Lippmann states, and is really "a transfiguration" of an event. That event can never be understood without knowing far more than we are likely to know about the way that it has been seen and by whom. In the ordinary course of events the public will not get the truth from "the words . . . in their newspapers."[16] In fact, if derived from the newspapers, our opinions will be both materially and morally wrong. In 1924–1925 *The Great Gatsby* revived a number of points in the dialogue by insisting on the presence in its text of other and subverting texts. In 1926, John Dewey capped the argument: not only were "news" and truth in a conscious, adversarial relationship, so were "news" and the novel. Media could not hope for "intellectual form," and the matter of reportage needed to be restated (in the form of "art" or fiction) if only to be understood:

> "News" signifies something which has just happened, and which is new just because it deviates from the old and regular. But its *meaning* depends upon relation to what it imports, to what its social consequences are. This import cannot be determined unless the new is placed in relation to the old, to what has happened and been integrated into the course of events. Without coordination and consecutiveness, events are not events, but mere occurrences, intrusions; an event implies that out of which a happening proceeds.

Dewey concludes that it is the function of the novel (and also of American poetry and drama) to state "news" in a way that is more absolute and "real." In fact, he added, "Artists have always been the real purveyors of news, for it is not the outward happening in itself which is new, but the kindling by it of emotion, perception and appreciation."[17] As far as Dewey could see, the mere public statement of an event had no special meaning. Whatever latent meaning there might be in an event was often corrupted by the tactics of media. Fitzgerald was uneasy not only about his audience but about the power of the press to debase public taste. His argument extends the speculation, in *This Side of Paradise,* that greatness is the special target of public opinion. And it includes, I think, his persistent worry that this novel would be misunderstood by a mass audience. "News" may provide the materials of Fitzgerald's art, but it also prevents that art from being expressed; it creates an audience that cannot tell the music from the noise.

By the end of the novel Nick faces the dilemma of making sense of discrete moments of experience. He must act on the basis of belief, must assert meanings. The materials available to him in the world of the early twentieth century had much to say about these things— to think of Eliot's Prufrock is to identify a figure who states but cannot solve the issue. And from *The Waste Land* (1922) to *The Sun Also Rises* (1926), the literary energies applied to the issue were enough to indicate its staying power. But throughout the last decade of the nineteenth century and the first decade of the twentieth it had also been widely argued that we can make experience meaningful. I do not want to imply that this view is simply characteristic of the Roosevelt era. Whenever possible, textual connections should be made. We should be alert to Fitzgerald's deployment of common terms implying, among other important connections, the conflict of confusion and "order"; that of consciousness and "drift"; and that of action and resistance.

Only by an effort of the will do we first arouse consciousness, then determine a course of action, then apply our moral resources to a conclusion. Nick Carraway begins in very nearly metaphysical uncertainty—certainly in psychological oblivion—but undertakes this necessary progression. He does not treat what he does ironically, the sharpest of differences between himself, Eliot, Hemingway, and others like Edmund Wilson who wanted to concede certain points about the cultural moment.

Fitzgerald has sensed the attractions in the early twenties of surrender to contemporary dejection—here is Edmund Wilson in a less than Coleridgean moment just as Jay Gatsby's story begins, in June 1922: "Among the familiar limited forms of history, fiction and thought and of the world about me as I have found it, I sometimes feel that the world is too small and its phenomena too petty and imperfect. . . . smothering in the past, brought up against the blankness of the future."[18] Wilson was quick enough to attack Fitzgerald's sentimentality, but there are also ironic forms of sentimentality. Fitzgerald is at his strongest when he states and solves issues at the end of his narrative. Nick Carraway may feel somewhat like Wilson about the American "world" and a great deal like Prufrock about the larger world, but toward the end of his narrative he does not act as if he did. I think that in this case a narrator does become the hero of his own life:

> I found myself on Gatsby's side, and alone. From the moment I telephoned news of the catastrophe to West Egg Village, every surmise about him, and every practical question, was referred to me. At first I was surprised and confused; then as he lay in his house and didn't move or breathe or speak hour upon hour it grew upon me that I was responsible, because no one else was interested—interested, I mean, with that intense personal interest to which everyone has some vague right at the end. [127–28]

The reader engages at this point discrepancies between ideas and acts and states of mind. What Nick does is heroic—but also demeaning. The last chapter gives him no opportunity to state a large moral principle. He will not be seen, like Tom Buchanan, defending civilization at the barricades. Nick seems, in fact, unable to state grand principles, preferring to rely on the civility that is so large a part of his stated character. He will not be forced into accusations, nor does he want precisely to state why he does what he does. But he will in his quiet way reaffirm the meaning of words he has inherited that give a moral dimension to the ideas of friendship, loyalty, and identity.

What Nick accomplishes is important, affecting, and full of value. Yet he is never allowed to confront any specific opposition or to fix on a particular thing that shows the importance of a single idea. There is a reason. His grinding moral determination is cast in the language of probabilities. Most moral decision actually occurs in this way, in the face of indifference rather than opposition, the myth being that not of Prometheus but of Sisyphus.

The novel's end involves Nick Carraway against unconsciousness. His adversaries simply refuse to be engaged. He is at the lowest moment of any conceivable action, because what he does could so easily pass unnoticed. Silence is in fact his temptation. Few things in fiction, or in life, are more admirable than Fitzgerald's depiction of the way that act proceeds from idea and against nothing in particular. And yet what he does is deeply familiar. We recall its reiterated statement in the Public Philosophy, the reminders that heroism is constituted of moments of not particularly heroic decision. Out of consciousness proceeds intention, and out of will proceeds act.

We should not be surprised to see the victory of act over "confused" reality: the affirmation that something must be done. Nick's arousal into consciousness follows the conviction imprinted by William James into American cultural debate (reemphasized, to give Puritanism its due) that both thought and action were the product of conscious responsibility, of "Will" in capital letters. James's ideas were continually reinvoked, by Royce, by Dewey, by Lippmann, by Eliot, even by one Horace Tarbox. Among those ideas was representative heroism. Mr. Gatz may not know exactly what great men do besides get rich and build up the country, but Nick Carraway certainly does. Perhaps William James can say something about Nick's understanding of the exemplary life he has seen unfold. Let us emphasize the importance, James wrote, of "picking out from history our heroes, and communing with their kindred spirits—in imagining as strongly as possible what differences their individualities brought about in this world, whilst its surface was still plastic in their hands . . . each one of us may best fortify and inspire what creative energy may lie in his own soul."[19] The relationship between act and witness is especially important: to see "resolute moral energy, no matter how inarticulate or unequipped with learning its owner may be, extorts from us a respect we should never pay *were we not satisfied that the essential root of human personality lay there.*"[20] Clearly, Gatsby is no Saint Joan. But as a hero for a moment, he is what we have. And one thing that he accomplishes is to pass on to Nick, hence to us, a sense of the *use* of consciousness and creative energies.

James was infinitely tactical, leaving instructions to his and the next generation on every step of the progression from mindless fatalism and "nerveless will" to active consciousness. He once described an idea important to the last chapters of Fitzgerald's text, the moment of decision. Every moment of thought (his subject was the drudgery of writing itself) is liable to become "an *escape*" from action if we allow it. "The thing has to be conquered every minute afresh by an act."[21] That attitude and concentration on discipline lies behind the grim, quixotic, and intensely repetitive sequence of events in the last chapter. It is an inherited attitude, powerfully stated a few years later in a line from "Babylon Revisited" that I have cited earlier, in which Charlie Wales wants not only to jump back a whole generation but to trust in character again. To elide a generation is to return to the world objectified by William James.

Nick, who belongs unwillingly to that past generation and its belief in "character," refuses the temptations of silence. He not only handles every practical question but *brings to consciousness* the meaning of experience, phoning Daisy, tracing Wolfsheim, hearing what Gatsby would have said, listening to the interminable Mr. Gatz, settling with Jordan, telling Tom, finally, what he is.

It is important to see that Fitzgerald at this point is engaging the conventional language of his moment. His text takes issue with social-historical similes and metaphors, although he knows about purgation by flooding waters and about leaving things to the providence of history and other forms of intellectuals' sentimentality. But Nick states with a sense of formal recognition of idea in image, "I wanted to leave things in order and not just trust that obliging and indifferent sea to sweep my refuse away" (138). The language is stubborn and resistant. Fitzgerald's ending leaves us with consciousness usefully deployed. As John Dewey had stated in the *New Republic* (April 12, 1922) just before the moment of this story, what matters in moral decisions are consequences and what emphatically does not matter are "sweeping and easy generalizations."[22] There is something else that is useful in this essay, and I will return to it momentarily.

The idea of "order" underlies Nick's purpose. James thought that "order," a key word in his own terminology, was the purpose of existence; we can see it in more circumscribed form as the purpose of writing itself. James may be given the last word on that metaphor revived so many times by so many writers of Fitzgerald's moment but significantly rejected at the novel's end: "Shipwreck and dissolution are not the absolutely final things."[23]

None of what Nick does at the end is necessary unless you feel that you must conquer "every minute afresh by an act." The last chapter is an endless sequence of failures and embarrassments. The tone is calculated to humiliate. Experience repeats itself moment by moment: Nick must stand outside an office and listen to lies from everyday life. He must wait by a ringing telephone and be put off by flunkies. At this point even the miserable Klipspringer comes to social life, anxious not to miss a picnic for a funeral, the Duc de Guermantes in small type. The scenes are played in social diminuendo, all of them giving Nick a chance to take advantage of the same fictions as those who prove now to be his adversaries. He is given every chance to lie or to surrender because it means seeing things only as others see them. It matters greatly that Gatsby's largeness of tone and temper, and Nick's own largeness of conscience be framed by littleness. There is a circle of connection in the 1922 essay by John Dewey that I have just mentioned: the belief in human consequences compels "attention to details, to particulars, it safeguards one from seclusion in universals; one is obliged, as William James was always saying, to get down from noble aloofness into the muddy stream of concrete things."[24]

In "The Offshore Pirate" (1920) Ardita Farnam has thought about life in terms of resisting hopeless odds: "I began to see," she says, "that in all my idols in the past some manifestation of courage had unconsciously been the thing that attracted me. I began separating courage from the other things of life. All sorts of courage—the beaten, bloody prize-fighter coming up for more."[25] She understands that resistance is sometimes all we have. As a first-rate book about Fitzgerald states, his work in the early twenties is about "the power of the individual," and it is expressed in terms of "his strong moral sense."[26] But it is also about lost causes. It is infiltrated with the language of James and Royce and Dewey about moral experience. It calls us back to the past generation—which is

Fitzgerald's lost generation of this century. The end sentence of this novel describes resistance, not acquiescence, navigation and not drift. I think that its key word is "against." There is more than one American hero in this story.

NOTES

Introduction

1. F. Scott Fitzgerald, "Early Success," in *The Crack-Up*, ed. Edmund Wilson (New York: New Directions, 1945), 87.

2. F. Scott Fitzgerald, *The Short Stories of F. Scott Fitzgerald*, ed. Matthew J. Bruccoli (New York: Charles Scribner's Sons, 1989), 619.

3. Ibid., 3–24.

4. See *This Side of Paradise* (1920; reprint, New York: Collier, 1986), 213–16; William James, "Great Men and Their Environment," in *The Will to Believe and Other Essays in Popular Philosophy*, ed. Frederick H. Burkhardt (Cambridge, Mass.: Harvard University Press, 1979), 163ff.; George Santayana, *The Life of Reason* (New York: Charles Scribner's Sons, 1905), 119–22.

5. Josiah Royce, "Loyalty and Insight," in *William James and Other Essays on the Philosophy of Life* (New York: Macmillan, 1911), 72–73.

6. Kern, *The Culture of Time and Space, 1880–1918* (Cambridge, Mass.: Harvard University Press, 1983), 182. Kern cites Lippmann's *Drift and Mastery* (1914).

7. H. L. Mencken, "A Glance Ahead," in *A Mencken Chrestomathy* (New York: Vintage, 1982), 158. See also "American Culture" (1920), 178–83, a discussion, among other things, of upper-class fearfulness and resentment masquerading as genuine aristocracy.

8. Walter Lippmann, *A Preface to Morals* (New York: Macmillan, 1929), 17.

9. See the discussion of "The Ice Palace" in Alice Hall Petry, *Fitzgerald's Craft of Short Fiction* (Tuscaloosa: University of Alabama Press, 1989), 43ff.

10. All citations are to F. Scott Fitzgerald, *The Great Gatsby*, ed. Matthew J. Bruccoli (Cambridge: Cambridge University Press, 1991).

11. George Santayana, *Character and Opinion in the United States* (1920; reprint, New York: Doubleday Anchor, 1956), 108.

12. Ibid., 109.

13. See Kern, *The Culture of Time and Space, 1880–1918*, 28–29.

14. From Harry Levin's "*Madame Bovary:* The Cathedral and the Hospital," reprinted in Gustave Flaubert, *Madame Bovary,* ed. Leo Bersani (New York: Bantam, 1981), 362.

1. Old Values and New Times

1. See Paul Fussell, *The Great War and Modern Memory* (New York: Oxford University Press, 1975), and Samuel Hynes, *A War Imagined* (New York: Atheneum, 1991).

2. Frederick James Smith, "Fitzgerald, Flappers, and Fame," in *The Romantic Egoists,* ed. Matthew J. Bruccoli, Scottie Fitzgerald Smith, and Joan P. Kerr (New York: Charles Scribner's Sons, 1974), 79.

3. A locus classicus for the criticism of the novel (and the myth) of seeking one's fortune appears in Lionel Trilling's "The Princess Casamassima," in *The Liberal Imagination* (New York: Viking, 1950), 61–64.

4. See John B. Chambers, *The Novels of F. Scott Fitzgerald* (London: Macmillan, 1989): as Nick arrives on East Egg the text displays "the dominance of images of power, paralysis, and sterility" (110). See also Milton R. Stern's essay on *The Great Gatsby* in *The Golden Moment* (Urbana: University of Illinois Press, 1970), 200–203. Stern describes "the sense of spiritual inanition" governing the scene.

5. *The Interpretation of Dreams* went through seven editions from 1899 to 1922. See the edition of James Strachey (New York: Avon, 1963), xii–xiii.

6. Reprinted in Sigmund Spaeth, *Read 'Em and Weep* (New York: Arco, 1959), 226–27.

7. See John Keats, "Ode to a Nightingale," in *Complete Poems,* ed. Jack Stillinger (Cambridge, Mass.: Belknap, 1982), 279–81; Percy Bysshe Shelley, "The Woodman and the Nightingale," in *The Complete Poetical Works,* ed. Thomas Hutchinson (London: Oxford University Press, 1956), 562–64; T. S. Eliot, "Sweeney Among the Nightingales," in *Collected Poems, 1909–1962* (New York: Harcourt, Brace & World, 1963), 50. The phrase "dull oblivion" comes from Shelley.

8. The *Vanity Fair* rubric is in all of its numbers; the *Saturday Evening Post* is quoted from the number of November 11, 1922.

9. See the semimilitary outfits for women from 1921 to 1926 in JoAnne Olian, *Authentic French Fashions of the Twenties* (New York: Dover, 1990), 28, 108–109.

10. See F. Scott Fitzgerald, "Handle with Care," in *The Crack-Up,* ed. Edmund Wilson (New York: New Directions, 1945): "The old dream of being an entire man in the Goethe-Byron-Shaw tradition, with an opulent American touch . . . has been relegated to the junk heap" (84).

11. A. E. Elmore, "*The Great Gatsby* as Well Wrought Urn," in *Modern American Fiction: Form and Function,* ed. Thomas Daniel Young (Baton Rouge: Louisiana State University Press, 1989), 62–63.

12. See Gillian Beer, *Darwin's Plots: Evolutionary Narrative in Darwin, George Eliot, and Nineteenth-Century Fiction* (London: Ark, 1983) throughout, and also George Levine, *Darwin and the Novelists: Patterns of Science in Victorian Fiction* (Cambridge, Mass.: Harvard University Press, 1988).

13. See George Cotkin, *William James, Public Philosopher* (Baltimore: Johns Hopkins University Press, 1990), 91. What Jacques Barzun calls "The Reign of William and Henry" coincided with the first eighteen years of Fitzgerald's life. See *A Stroll with William James* (New York: Harper & Row, 1983), 181–226.

14. Barzun, *A Stroll with William James,* 1–5.

15. Ibid., 222.

16. H. L. Mencken, "Professor Veblen," in *A Mencken Chrestomathy* (New York: Vintage Books, 1982), 266. Originally published in *Prejudices: First Series,* 1919.

17. Cited by Barzun, *A Stroll with William James,* 297. See the discussion of James's reputation on 296ff. *Civilization in the United States* (New

York: Harcourt Brace, 1922) was edited by Harold Stearns. Its subtitle, *An Inquiry by Thirty Americans,* indicates the scope of its coverage of American arts, letters, science, etc.

18. William James, *Pragmatism* (Cleveland: Meridian, 1907), 26.

19. William James, "Is Life Worth Living?" in *The Will to Believe and Other Essays in Popular Philosophy,* ed. Frederick H. Burkhardt (Cambridge, Mass.: Harvard University Press, 1979), 34–56.

20. James, *The Will to Believe,* 159.

21. See Ronald Berman, *"The Great Gatsby" and Modern Times* (Urbana: University of Illinois Press, 1994), 20ff.

22. H. L. Mencken, *A Mencken Chrestomathy,* 169–77.

23. Walter Lippmann's *Public Opinion* was one of the great texts of 1922. It came out, in part, in the *New Republic* in the spring of that year, just as the events of Fitzgerald's novel begin, and it argues against current ideologies of resentment.

24. See Hannah Arendt, "Race-Thinking Before Racism," in *The Origins of Totalitarianism* (Cleveland: Meridian, 1958), 158–84.

25. Morton White, "The Philosopher and the Metropolis in America," in *Pragmatism and the American Mind* (New York: Oxford University Press, 1973), 11–30.

26. See the essays in *A Second Mencken Chrestomathy,* ed. Terry Teachout (New York: Alfred A. Knopf, 1995), 179–92.

27. Quoted in Morton White, "The Philosopher and the Metropolis in America," in *Pragmatism and the American Mind,* 22.

28. Ibid.

29. John Dewey, "William James in 1926, " in *The Later Works, 1925–1953,* 2 vols., ed. Jo Ann Boydston (Carbondale: Southern Illinois University Press, 1984), 2:158–62.

30. See White, *Pragmatism and the American Mind,* 22–24.

31. John Dewey, "Experience, Nature, and Art," in *The Later Works, 1925–1953,* 1:273–74.

32. Josiah Royce, *The World and the Individual: Second Series* (New York: Dover, 1901), 335–75. Revised and extended in *The Basic Writings of Josiah Royce,* 2 vols., ed. John J. McDermott (Chicago: University of Chicago Press, 1969), 1:421ff.

33. Cotkin, *William James, Public Philosopher,* 111.

34. Barzun, *A Stroll with William James,* 184. Barzun quotes James from *Essays in Radical Empiricism* (New York: Longmans, 1911), 39–40.

2 . D E M O S

1. George Santayana, *Character and Opinion in the United States* (1920; reprint, New York: Doubleday Anchor, 1956), 102–18.

2. See the review of *The Waste Land* references by Jackson R. Bryer, "Four Decades of Fitzgerald Studies: The Best and the Brightest," *Twentieth Century Literature* 26 (Summer 1980): 263.

3. William James, *Pragmatism* (Cleveland: Meridian, 1907), 24.

4. See Walter Lippmann, *A Preface to Morals* (New York: Macmillan, 1929), 9.

5. Sir Arthur Conan Doyle, "The Valley of Fear," in *The Final Adventures of Sherlock Holmes,* ed. Edgar W. Smith (New York: Heritage, 1952), 1463–69.

6. Fitzgerald seems to have mined Doyle for ideas and even for a title: "The Darkest Hour" is a chapter heading in this Sherlock Holmes story; and "In the Darkest Hour" is the title of a story that Fitzgerald hoped to make into something larger. Fitzgerald's story begins with a view of yet another valley in "ruins." See Matthew J. Bruccoli's edition of *The Price Was High* (New York: Harcourt Brace Jovanovich, 1979), 513.

7. Santayana, *Character and Opinion in the United States,* 108.

8. For views on consumer society differing from my own, see Patricia Bizzell, "Pecuniary Emulation of the Mediator in *The Great Gatsby,*" in *Major Literary Characters: Gatsby,* ed. Harold Bloom (New York: Chelsea House, 1991), 113–20; and Richard Godden, "Glamour on the Turn," 121–36. These two essays are about money and commodities in the novel.

9. The quotation from the *New York Times Book Review* of October 18, 1925, appears in Michael Reynolds, *Hemingway: The American Homecoming* (Cambridge: Blackwell, 1992), 4.

10. See Harry Levin, "Observations on the Style of Ernest Hemingway," in *Memories of the Moderns* (New York: New Directions, 1980): "If we regard the adjective as a luxury, decorative more often than functional, we

can well understand why Hemingway doesn't cultivate it. But, assuming that the sentence derives its energy from the verb, we are in for a shock if we expect his verbs to be numerous or varied or emphatic. His usage supports C. K. Ogden's argument that verb-forms are disappearing from English grammar. Without much self-deprivation, Hemingway could get along on the so-called 'operators' of Basic English, the sixteen monosyllabic verbs that stem from movements of the body. The substantive verb *to be* is predominant, characteristically introduced by an expletive" (96).

11. Amy Kaplan, *The Social Construction of American Realism* (Chicago: University of Chicago Press, 1988), 12.

12. Judith Fryer, *Felicitous Space* (Chapel Hill: University of North Carolina Press, 1986), 49.

13. Kaplan, *The Social Construction of American Realism,* 13.

14. See the special fiftieth anniversary edition: *Twentieth Century Advertising and the Economy of Abundance,* April 30, 1980, 87.

15. Robert S. Lynd and Helen Merrell Lynd, *Middletown: A Study in Modern American Culture* (New York: Harcourt Brace, 1929), 475.

16. Ibid., 266.

17. Ibid., 240.

18. See Sinclair Lewis, *Babbitt* (1922; reprint, New York: Signet, 1980), 183–84, on "the worship of new gods." Eunice Littlefield, the girl next door, wants "to be a cinema actress. She did not merely attend the showing of every 'feature film;' she also read the motion-picture magazines . . . monthlies and weeklies gorgeously illustrated with portraits of young women who had recently been manicure girls" (ibid.).

19. Ibid., 120–21.

20. F. Scott Fitzgerald, *The Crack-Up,* ed. Edmund Wilson (New York: New Directions, 1945), 14.

21. Wharton, *The Age of Innocence* (1920; reprint, New York: Collier, 1987), 352–53.

22. Walter Lippmann, *Public Opinion* (New York: Macmillan, 1922), 73–74.

23. John Dewey, "Existence as Precarious and as Stable," in *The Later Works, 1925–1953,* 2 vols., ed. Jo Ann Boydston (Carbondale: Southern Illinois University Press, 1981), 1:54–55.

24. Walter Lippmann, *A Preface to Morals,* 64–65.

25. Barzun, *A Stroll with William James* (New York: Harper & Row, 1983), 217.

26. See Ronald Paulson, *Hogarth: His Life, Art, and Times* (New Haven: Yale University Press, 1974), 306.

3. COMMUNITY AND CROWD

1. See George Santayana, *Character and Opinion in the United States* (1920; reprint, New York: Doubleday Anchor, 1956), 108–10.

2. See John Milton Cooper, Jr., "The Twenties Begin," in *Pivotal Decades: The United States, 1900–1920* (New York: W. W. Norton, 1990), 357–76. Harding's "Normalcy" campaign of 1920 stressed "an ingenious blend of old and new" (370). It was "backward-looking" but allowed for "progress." Any future "benefits" were firmly based on "the values of the past."

3. George Santayana, "Free Society," in *The Life of Reason* (New York: Charles Scribner's Sons, 1905), 137–59.

4. F. Scott Fitzgerald, "Echoes of the Jazz Age," in *The Crack-Up,* ed. Edmund Wilson (New York: New Directions, 1945), 15.

5. Ernest H. Lockridge, ed., *Twentieth Century Interpretations of "The Great Gatsby"* (Englewood Cliffs: Prentice-Hall, 1968), 5–8.

6. Arnold Weinstein, "Fiction as Greatness: The Case of Gatsby," *Novel* 19 (Fall 1985): 26.

7. M. A. Klug, "Horns of Manichaeus: The Conflict of Art and Experience in *The Great Gatsby* and *The Sun Also Rises,*" *Essays in Literature* 12 (Spring 1985): 113.

8. Ibid.

9. Park Honan, *Jane Austen: Her Life* (New York: Fawcett Columbine, 1987), 87.

10. Ibid., 88.

11. F. Scott Fitzgerald, "May Day," in *The Short Stories of F. Scott Fitzgerald,* ed. Matthew J. Bruccoli (New York: Charles Scribner's Sons, 1989), 113.

12. F. Scott Fitzgerald, *The Short Stories of F. Scott Fitzgerald,* 25.

13. "The Jelly-Bean," in *The Short Stories of F. Scott Fitzgerald,* 147.

14. "Metropolis," in *A Second Mencken Chrestomathy,* ed. Terry Teachout (New York: Alfred A. Knopf, 1995), 189, 190. From *Prejudices: Sixth Series,* 1927.

15. "Totentanz," in *A Second Mencken Chrestomathy,* 181. Mencken's essay (from *Prejudices: Fourth Series,* 1924) reiterates the theme of the metropolis as "Babylon," in which women are for sale and in which "social organization" follows marketplace demand.

16. See R. Berman, *"The Great Gatsby" and Modern Times* (Urbana: University of Illinois Press, 1994), 8–9, 85–93.

17. "Metropolis," in *A Second Mencken Chrestomathy,* 188.

18. Gerald Early, "The Lives of Jazz," *American Literary History* 5 (Spring 1993): 130. Fitzgerald at the time (February 1924) was still in Great Neck.

19. Gerald Early, "The Lives of Jazz," 132. For a review of jazz in the first quarter of the century, see Kathy J. Ogren, *The Jazz Revolution: Twenties America and the Meaning of Jazz* (New York: Oxford University Press, 1989). For a short, sharp attack on Whiteman's social style, see Edmund Wilson, "The Problem of the Higher Jazz," in *The American Earthquake* (New York: Farrar Straus Giroux, 1958): Whiteman "has refined and disciplined his orchestra to a point at which, one would think, his old clientele of dancers and diners could only be embarrassed by it" (114). For a classic of scholarship that outlines Fitzgerald's use of lyrics, see Ruth Prigozy, " 'Poor Butterfly': F. Scott Fitzgerald and Popular Music," in the annual *Prospects* 2 (1976): 41–67.

20. See H. L. Mencken "Totentanz," in *A Second Mencken Chrestomathy,* passim.

21. Page Smith, *Redeeming the Time* (New York: McGraw-Hill, 1987), 9.

22. Ibid.

23. John Dewey, "Search for the Public," in *The Later Works, 1925–1952,* 2 vols., ed. Jo Ann Boydston (Carbondale: Southern Illinois University Press, 1981, 1984), 2:250.

24. William James, "Humanism and Truth," in *Selected Papers on Philosophy* (London: J. M. Dent & Sons, 1917), 224. The essay was first published in 1904.

25. John E. Smith, *The Spirit of American Philosophy* (New York: Oxford University Press, 1963), 80–114.

26. F. Scott Fitzgerald, "Echoes of the Jazz Age," in *The Crack-Up,* 14.

27. Geoffrey Perrett, *America in the Twenties* (New York: Touchstone, 1982), 147.

28. Havelock Ellis, *The Dance of Life* (Boston: Houghton Mifflin, 1923), 277–83.

29. F. Scott Fitzgerald, "Echoes of the Jazz Age," in *The Crack-Up,* ed. Wilson, 15.

30. See *W. B. Yeats: The Poems,* ed. Richard J. Finneran (New York: Macmillan, 1983), 206–10.

31. John E. Smith, *The Spirit of American Philosophy,* 92–93.

4. Mixed Democracy

1. Robert Emmet Long, *The Achieving of "The Great Gatsby"* (Lewisburg: Bucknell University Press, 1979), 140–43.

2. F. Scott Fitzgerald, *The Short Stories of F. Scott Fitzgerald,* ed. Matthew J. Bruccoli (New York: Charles Scribner's Sons, 1989), 182.

3. Ibid., 200–201.

4. John Dewey, "Search for the Great Community," in *The Later Works, 1925–1953,* 2 vols., ed. Jo Ann Boydston (Carbondale: Southern Illinois University Press, 1981, 1984), 2:341.

5. Henry James, *The American Scene* (Bloomington: Indiana University Press, 1907), 133. James uses the word "phantasmagoric" twice in addition in this passage.

6. Charles Merz, *The Great American Band Wagon* (New York: Literary Guild, 1928), 235–36.

7. André Le Vot describes self-invention through naming in 1924. At the parties of Gerald and Sara Murphy in Antibes attended by the Fitzgeralds, Rudolph Valentino brought "his wife, Natasha Rambova. . . . Her real name was Winifred Hudnut and she was the adopted daughter of an American millionaire, but she had been so influenced by her romantic Russian friend Alla Nazimova . . . that she chose a Russian name that chimed more sweetly with the name Rudolph—which was also an invention." Natasha's

"phantom name" elevated the style of mere democracy. From *F. Scott Fitzgerald* (Garden City: Doubleday, 1983), 204.

8. George Santayana, "Democracy," in *The Life of Reason* (New York: Charles Scribner's Sons, 1905), 127. This edition was reprinted in 1919.

9. Walter Lippmann, *Public Opinion* (New York: Macmillan, 1922), 274–75.

10. Joseph Wood Krutch, *The Modern Temper* (New York: Harcourt Brace, 1929), 6.

11. Ibid., 5.

12. See, for example, Marius Bewley, "Scott Fitzgerald's Criticism of America," and Robert Ornstein, "Scott Fitzgerald's Fable of East and West," in *Twentieth Century Interpretations of "The Great Gatsby,"* ed. Ernest Lockridge (Englewood Cliffs: Prentice-Hall, 1968), 37–60.

13. Alexis de Tocqueville, "How The Americans Combat the Effects of Individualism by Free Institutions," in *Democracy in America,* ed. J. P. Mayer (New York: Anchor, 1969), 512. Emphasis added.

14. Alexis de Tocqueville, *Democracy in America,* 535–38.

15. Ibid., 537.

16. Henry James, *The American Scene,* 72–73.

17. Anti-Semitism was commonplace, but conditions were changing. In its first year of publication *Time* covered Jewish authors, scientists, artists, and others in respectful depth. The cover for September 17, 1923, featured Israel Zangwill; the story mentioned Brandeis, Einstein, Henry Morgenthau, Stephen S. Wise, and others who exemplified not only accomplishment but responsible citizenship here and abroad.

18. Sklar, *F. Scott Fitzgerald: The Last Laocoon* (New York: Oxford University Press, 1967), 183.

19. See Kenneth Keniston's essay "Youth as a Stage of Life," in *Readings in Child Development,* ed. Harry Munsinger (New York: Holt, Rinehart & Winston, 1975), 243–57.

5. INDIVIDUALISM RECONSIDERED

1. F. Scott Fitzgerald, *This Side of Paradise* (1920; reprint, New York: Collier, 1986), 154. These lines from the ending of Fitzgerald's "Princeton—

The Last Day" (1917) were originally in verse. See Matthew J. Bruccoli, *Some Sort of Epic Grandeur* (New York: Harcourt Brace Jovanovich, 1981), 72.

2. Ibid.

3. Cedric H. Whitman, "Fire and Other Elements," *Homer and the Heroic Tradition* (New York: W. W. Norton, 1958), 129.

4. Fitzgerald, *This Side of Paradise,* 214–15.

5. William James, "The Sentiment of Rationality," *The Will to Believe,* ed. Frederick H. Burkhardt (Cambridge, Mass.: Harvard University Press, 1979), 89.

6. Fitzgerald, *This Side of Paradise,* 215.

7. Hannah Arendt, *The Human Condition* (Chicago: University of Chicago Press, 1958), 42–43.

8. W. H. Auden, "The Poet & The City," *The Dyer's Hand* (New York: Vintage, 1962), 80–83.

9. Robert F. Whitman, *Shaw and the Play of Ideas* (Ithaca: Cornell University Press, 1977), 204.

10. Bernard Shaw, *Saint Joan* (New York: Penguin, 1924), 77.

11. Robert F. Whitman, *Shaw and the Play of Ideas,* 270–71.

12. This passage from "Is Life Worth Living?" was cited in George Cotkin, *William James, Public Philosopher* (Baltimore: Johns Hopkins University Press, 1990), 91–93. I have relied on this book for my discussion of James. For the influence of the fiction of Frank Norris and the criticism of H. L. Mencken on the idea of moral energies, particularly of the "self-induced paralysis of the moral will," see James W. Tuttleton's "Seeing Slightly Red: Fitzgerald's 'May Day,'" in *The Short Stories of F. Scott Fitzgerald,* ed. Jackson R. Bryer (Madison: University of Wisconsin Press, 1982), 183–86.

13. This passage from "Talks to Students" was cited by Cotkin, 92.

14. This passage from "The Energies of Men" was cited by Cotkin, 93. Cotkin, however, refers to its later title, "The Powers of Men." In its earlier form this was a famous lecture given at Columbia University in 1906. My next citation will refer directly to James's text.

15. William James, "The Energies of Men," in *Selected Papers on Philosophy* (London: J. M. Dent & Sons, 1917), 53.

16. Ibid., 57.

17. William James, "The Dilemma of Determinism," in *The Will to Believe,* 114–40. Cited passages: 124, 131ff.

18. Hannah Arendt, *The Human Condition,* 311. This citation is from the discussion of "The Principle of Happiness" (305ff.), which Arendt considers a form of egoism masquerading as philosophy.

19. F. Scott Fitzgerald, "Rags Martin-Jones and the Pr———nce of W———les," in *The Short Stories of F. Scott Fitzgerald,* ed. Matthew J. Bruccoli (New York: Charles Scribner's Sons, 1989), 273–88.

20. Alexis de Tocqueville, "Why the Americans Are Often So Restless in the Midst of Prosperity," in *Democracy in America,* ed. J. P. Mayer (New York: Anchor Books, 1969), 538.

21. H. L. Mencken had a clear idea of why the quest was bound to fail. Set against our national mythology of equality was the admiration of "status." Mobility aspires to aristocracy: "the rich peasant becomes a planter and the father of doctors of philosophy, and the servant girl enters the movies and acquires the status of a princess of the blood, and the petty attorney becomes a legislator and statesman, and Schmidt turns into Smith . . . and all of us Yankees creep up, up, up." But, Mencken adds, it all must be done insidiously and pianissimo, "lest the portcullis fall and the whole enterprise go to pot." There is the extremely interesting reminder that we need "protective coloration" lest we be unmasked by those who have arrived before us—and the primary national social skill must be imitation. From "The Pushful American," in *A Second Mencken Chrestomathy,* ed. Terry Teachout (New York: Alfred A. Knopf, 1995), 15. Originally published as the preface to *The American Credo* by Mencken and George Jean Nathan in 1920.

22. Otto Harbach and Louis A. Hirsch, "The Love Nest," in *The Legal Fake Book* (Warner Brothers, 1979), 181. From the musical comedy *Mary* (1920).

23. *Dear Scott/Dear Max: The Fitzgerald-Perkins Correspondence,* ed. John Kuehl and Jackson Bryer (New York: Charles Scribner's Sons, 1971), 85.

24. John Dryden, *The Poems of John Dryden,* 4 vols., ed. James Kinsley (Oxford: Clarendon Press, 1958), 3:1075–78.

25. Matthew J. Bruccoli, *Some Sort of Epic Grandeur,* 46ff.

26. Cited from a letter to Thomas Boyd in Matthew J. Bruccoli, *Some Sort of Epic Grandeur,* 197.

27. See Euripides, "Hippolytus," in *The Complete Greek Tragedies,* 4 vols., ed. David Grene and Richmond Lattimore (Chicago: University of Chicago Press, 1960), 3:220.

28. F. Scott Fitzgerald, "Basil and Cleopatra," in *The Short Stories of F. Scott Fitzgerald,* 447.

29. Harold E. Stearns, ed., *Civilization in the United States* (New York: Harcourt, Brace, 1922), 147–48.

6. ENERGIES

1. Walter Lippmann, *Public Opinion* (New York: Macmillan, 1922), 7.

2. F. Scott Fitzgerald, *This Side of Paradise* (1920; reprint, New York: Collier, 1986), 215.

3. Walter Lippmann, *Public Opinion,* 15–16. Lippmann cites William James's *Principles of Psychology.*

4. Ibid., 31.

5. William James, "The Social Value of the College-Bred," in *William James: Writings, 1902–1910,* ed. Bruce Kuklick (New York: Library of America, 1987), 1248–49.

6. Cited by John F. Kasson, *Amusing the Million: Coney Island at the Turn of the Century* (New York: Hill & Wang, 1978), 112. From Tilyou's "Human Nature with the Brakes Off; or, Why the Schoolma'am Walked into the Sea," *American Magazine* 94 (July 1922): 19, 21, 86, 92.

7. George Santayana, "Marginal Notes on Civilization in the United States," in *Santayana on America,* ed. Richard Colton Lyon (New York: Harcourt, Brace & World, 1968), 192. The essay was originally published in the *Dial* in June 1922.

8. William James, "The Energies of Men," *William James: Writings, 1902–1910,* 1239. This version of the essay varies considerably from the much earlier version that I have previously cited.

9. George Santayana, "William James," in *Character and Opinion in the United States* (1920; reprint, New York: Doubleday, 1956), 51.

10. See the discussion of Unitarianism in the opening chapters of Eric Sigg's *The American T. S. Eliot* (Cambridge: Cambridge University Press, 1989).

11. See the discussion of Eliot and Babbitt in Martin Scofield, *T. S. Eliot: The Poems* (Cambridge: Cambridge University Press, 1988), 14–15.

12. Ibid., 15. The terminology went back (at least) as far as 1890, the year of publication of Horatio Alger's *Struggling Upward*.

13. George Cotkin, *William James, Public Philosopher* (Baltimore: Johns Hopkins University Press, 1990), 106.

14. Samuel Hynes, *A War Imagined* (New York: Atheneum, 1991), 248.

15. George Santayana, *The Life of Reason* (New York: Charles Scribner's Sons, 1905), 125.

16. Ibid., 100.

17. Ibid.

18. William James, *The Will to Believe and Other Essays in Popular Philosophy,* ed. Frederick H. Burkhardt (Cambridge, Mass.: Harvard University Press, 1979), passim.

19. William James, "Is Life Worth Living?" in *The Will to Believe,* 34.

20. William James, "The Sentiment of Rationality," in *The Will to Believe,* 74.

21. William James, *The Will to Believe,* 24–25.

22. "Drift" is one of the fundamental metaphors used by Walter Lippmann. The term applies specifically to the morally and existentially unconscious life of most Americans. Its opposite, "mastery," not only means "the substitution of conscious intention for unconscious striving" but defines what ought to be our *national* purpose: "Civilization, it seems to me, is just this constant effort to introduce plan where there has been clash, and purpose into the jungles of disordered growth." The only way in which drift is turned into mastery is through "the light of consciousness." That is defined by Lippmann as the aggregate of recording, comparing, noting, reflecting— all components not only of the good philosophical life but of writing itself. From *Drift and Mastery: An Attempt to Diagnose the Current Unrest* (New York: Mitchell Kennerly, 1914), 268–69.

7. BELIEF AND WILL

1. Robert Emmet Long, *The Achieving of "The Great Gatsby"* (Lewisburg: Bucknell University Press, 1979), 152.

2. Thomas J. Stavola, *Scott Fitzgerald: Crisis in an American Identity* (London: Vision Press, 1979), 131.

3. Gary J. Scrimgeour, "Against *The Great Gatsby*," in *Twentieth Century Interpretations of "The Great Gatsby*," ed. Ernest Lockridge (Englewood Cliffs: Prentice-Hall, 1968), 73.

4. See William James, *Pragmatism* (Cleveland: Meridian, 1907): "Not only Walt Whitman could write 'who touches this book touches a man.' The books of all the great philosophers are like so many men" (35).

5. *The Basic Writings of Josiah Royce,* 2 vols., ed. John J. McDermott (Chicago: University of Chicago Press, 1969), 2:1015–37.

6. Ibid., 1035–36.

7. Ibid., 1037.

8. Royce, "The Philosophy of Loyalty," in *The Basic Writings of Josiah Royce,* 2:1009.

9. James, *Pragmatism,* 180.

10. Royce, "The Philosophy of Loyalty," *The Basic Writings of Josiah Royce,* 2:1008.

11. Walter Lippmann, *Drift and Mastery: An Attempt to Diagnose the Current Unrest* (New York: Mitchell Kennerley, 1914), 175.

12. Ibid., 176–77.

13. Walter Lippmann, *A Preface to Morals* (New York: Macmillan, 1929), 151.

14. Royce, "The Philosophy of Loyalty," *The Basic Writings of Josiah Royce,* 2:1023.

15. James, *Pragmatism,* 27.

16. T. S. Eliot, "The Waste Land," in *Collected Poems, 1909–1962* (New York: Harcourt, Brace & World, 1970), 53.

17. See the discussion of this concept by George Cotkin in *William James, Public Philosopher* (Baltimore: Johns Hopkins University Press, 1990), 99ff.

18. F. Scott Fitzgerald, "The Offshore Pirate," in *The Short Stories of F. Scott Fitzgerald,* ed. Matthew J. Bruccoli (New York: Charles Scribner's Sons, 1989), 88.

19. William James, "The Will," in *Selected Papers on Philosophy* (London: J. M. Dent & Sons, 1917), 67–75.

20. Janet Oppenheim, *Shattered Nerves* (New York: Oxford University Press, 1991), 293ff. Citation from 317. See also Tom Lutz on the moral restraint of anxiety in *American Nervousness, 1903* (Ithaca: Cornell University Press, 1991). A rare full-page ad in the *New Republic* of February 15, 1922, cites many contemporary opinions on "Outwitting Our Nerves." The task is to train our emotions, as has been "so wonderfully developed by Professor William James" (347).

21. *The Short Stories of F. Scott Fitzgerald*, 290–91.

22. Ibid., 293–94.

23. See T. J. Jackson Lears, *No Place of Grace* (Chicago: University of Chicago Press, 1994), 47–57.

24. William James, "The Will," in *Selected Papers on Philosophy*, 83.

8. RUINS AND ORDER

1. Matthew J. Bruccoli states in his "Explanatory Notes" section of the Cambridge edition of *The Great Gatsby* (Cambridge: Cambridge University Press, 1991) that "the time is August. Jonquils bloom in spring, hawthorn in late spring or very early summer, and plum trees in early spring" (197).

2. Alexis de Tocqueville, "Of Individualism in Democracies," in *Democracy in America,* ed. J. P. Mayer (New York: Anchor Books, 1969), 506 (first quotation); "Particular Effects of the Love of Physical Pleasures in Democratic Times," in *Democracy in America,* 533 (subsequent quotations).

3. Rodney Mims Cook, Jr., "Addison Mizner: America's Society Architect," *American Arts Quarterly* 10: 2 (Spring 1993): 26.

4. Ibid.

5. F. Scott Fitzgerald, *The Crack-Up,* ed. Edmund Wilson (New York: New Directions, 1945), 226–28.

6. F. Scott Fitzgerald, "Echoes of the Jazz Age," in *The Crack-Up,* ed. Wilson, 14–15.

7. Alexis de Tocqueville, "The Main Causes Tending to Maintain a Democratic Republic in the United States," in *Democracy in America,* 284.

8. Ibid.

9. Edith Wharton, "A Backward Glance," in *Edith Wharton: Novellas and Other Writings* (New York: Library of America, 1990), 781.

10. Ibid., 824–27.

11. Walter Lippmann, *A Preface to Morals* (New York: Macmillan, 1929), 19.

12. Edmund Wilson, *The Twenties,* ed. Leon Edel (New York: Farrar, Straus & Giroux, 1975), 121–23.

13. Ibid., 124. For a brief discussion of what constitutes the "values, ideals and dreams" of houses in *The Great Gatsby,* see Hilton Anderson, "From the Wasteland to East Egg: Houses in *The Great Gatsby," University of Mississippi Studies in English* 9 (1991): 114–18.

14. Matthew J. Bruccoli, *Some Sort of Epic Grandeur* (New York: Harcourt Brace Jovanovich, 1981), 184.

15. *A Mencken Chrestomathy* (New York: Vintage, 1982), 182–83.

16. Walter Lippmann, *Public Opinion* (1922; reprint, New York: Macmillan, 1961), 79, 91, 125.

17. John Dewey, "Search for the Great Community," in *The Later Works, 1925–1953,* 2 vols., ed. Jo Ann Boydston (Carbondale: Southern Illinois University Press, 1984), 2:347–50.

18. Edmund Wilson, *The Twenties,* 129–30.

19. William James, "The Importance of Individuals," in *The Will to Believe,* ed. Frederick H. Burkhardt (Cambridge, Mass.: Harvard University Press, 1979), 194.

20. William James, "Reflex Action and Theism," in *The Will to Believe,* 111. Emphasis added.

21. From an undated letter to Wincenty Lutoslawski, quoted in George Cotkin, *William James, Public Philosopher* (Baltimore: Johns Hopkins University Press, 1990), 101.

22. John Dewey, "Pragmatic America," *New Republic,* April 12, 1922, pp. 185–87 (quotation on p. 186).

23. These passages from *The Will to Believe* and *Varieties of Religious Experience* are quoted in Cotkin, 103.

24. John Dewey, "Pragmatic America," p. 186.

25. F. Scott Fitzgerald, "The Offshore Pirate," in *The Short Stories of F. Scott Fitzgerald,* ed. Matthew J. Bruccoli (New York: Charles Scribner's Sons, 1989), 87. The hand is the hand of Fitzgerald, but the voice is the voice of Teddy Roosevelt: "It is not the critic who counts; nor the man who points

out how the strong man stumbles, or where the doer of deeds could have done better. The credit belongs to the man who is actually in the arena, whose face is marred by dust and sweat and blood; who strives valiantly; . . . who spends himself in a worthy cause; who at the best knows in the end the triumph of high achievement, and who at the worst, if he fails, at least fails while daring greatly, so that his place shall never be with those cold and timid souls who know neither victory nor defeat." From *Theodore Roosevelt: An American Mind,* ed. Mario R. DiNunzio (New York: Penguin Books, 1994), xiii.

26. Alice Hall Petry, *Fitzgerald's Craft of Short Fiction* (Tuscaloosa: University of Alabama Press, 1989), 51.

BIBLIOGRAPHY

Allen, Frederick Lewis. *Only Yesterday.* 1931. Reprint. New York: Harper & Row, 1964.

Anderson, Hilton. "From the Wasteland to East Egg: Houses in *The Great Gatsby.*" *University of Mississippi Studies in English* 9 (1991): 114–18.

Arendt, Hannah. *The Human Condition.* Chicago: University of Chicago Press, 1958.

———. *The Origins of Totalitarianism.* Cleveland: Meridian, 1958.

Auden, W. H. "The Poet & The City." *The Dyer's Hand.* New York: Vintage, 1962.

Barzun, Jacques. *A Stroll with William James.* New York: Harper & Row, 1983.

Beer, Gillian. *Darwin's Plots: Evolutionary Narrative in Darwin, George Eliot, and Nineteenth-Century Fiction.* London: Ark, 1983.

Berman, Ronald. *"The Great Gatsby" and Modern Times.* Urbana: University of Illinois Press, 1994.

Bloom, Harold. *Major Literary Characters: Gatsby.* New York: Chelsea House, 1991.

Bruccoli, Matthew J. *Apparatus for F. Scott Fitzgerald's "The Great Gatsby" ["Under the Red, White, and Blue"].* Columbia: University of South Carolina Press, 1974.

———. *F. Scott Fitzgerald: A Life in Letters.* New York: Touchstone, 1994.

———. *Some Sort of Epic Grandeur.* New York: Harcourt Brace Jovanovich, 1981.

Bruccoli, Matthew J., with Scottie Fitzgerald and Joan P. Kerr, eds. *The Romantic Egoists.* New York: Charles Scribner's Sons, 1974.

Bryer, Jackson R. "Four Decades of Fitzgerald Studies: The Best and the Brightest." *Twentieth Century Literature* 26 (Summer 1980): 247–67.

———, ed. *The Short Stories of F. Scott Fitzgerald.* Madison: University of Wisconsin Press, 1982.

Chambers, John B. *The Novels of F. Scott Fitzgerald.* London: Macmillan, 1989.

Cook, Rodney Mims. "Addison Mizner: America's Society Architect." *American Arts Quarterly* 10 (Spring 1993): 26–29.

Cooper, John Milton, Jr. *Pivotal Decades: The United States, 1900–1920.* New York: W. W. Norton, 1990.

Cotkin, George. *William James, Public Philosopher.* Baltimore: Johns Hopkins University Press, 1990.

Dewey, John. *The Later Works, 1925–1953.* Edited by Jo Ann Boydston. 2 vols. Carbondale: Southern Illinois University Press, 1981, 1984.

Doyle, Sir Arthur Conan. *The Final Adventures of Sherlock Holmes.* Edited by Edgar W. Smith. New York: Heritage, 1952.

Dryden, John. *The Poems of John Dryden.* Edited by James Kinsley. 4 vols. Oxford: Clarendon Press, 1958.

Early, Gerald. "The Lives of Jazz." *American Literary History* 5 (Spring 1993): 129–46.

Ellis, Havelock. *The Dance of Life.* Boston: Houghton Mifflin, 1923.

Elmore, A. E. "*The Great Gatsby* as Well Wrought Urn." In *Modern American Fiction: Form and Function,* edited by Thomas Daniel Young. Baton Rouge: Louisiana State University Press, 1989.

Fitzgerald, F. Scott. *Afternoon of an Author.* New York: Charles Scribner's Sons, 1957.

———. *The Great Gatsby.* Edited by Matthew J. Bruccoli. 1925. Reprint. Cambridge: Cambridge University Press, 1991.

———. *The Price Was High.* Edited by Matthew J. Bruccoli. 1920. Reprint. New York: Harcourt Brace Jovanovich, 1979.

———. *The Short Stories of F. Scott Fitzgerald.* Edited by Matthew J. Bruccoli. New York: Charles Scribner's Sons, 1989.

———. *This Side of Paradise.* 1920. Reprint. New York: Collier, 1986.

Flaubert, Gustave. *Madame Bovary.* Edited by Leo Bersani. New York: Bantam, 1981.

Freud, Sigmund. *The Interpretation of Dreams.* New York: Avon, 1963.

Fryer, Judith. *Felicitous Space.* Chapel Hill: University of North Carolina Press, 1986.

Fussell, Paul. *The Great War and Modern Memory.* New York: Oxford University Press, 1975.

Harbach, Otto, and Louis A. Hirsch. "The Love Nest." In *The Legal Fake Book.* Warner Brothers, 1979.

Hobson, Fred. *Mencken: A Life.* New York: Random House, 1994.

Honan, Park. *Jane Austen: Her Life*. New York: Fawcett Columbine, 1987.

Hynes, Samuel. *A War Imagined*. New York: Atheneum, 1991.

James, Henry. *The American Scene*. Bloomington: Indiana University Press, 1907.

James, William. *Essays, Comments, and Reviews*. Edited by Frederick H. Burkhardt. Cambridge, Mass.: Harvard University Press, 1987.

———. *Essays in Philosophy*. Edited by Frederick H. Burkhardt. Cambridge, Mass.: Harvard University Press, 1978.

———. *Pragmatism*. Cleveland: Meridian, 1907.

———. *Selected Papers on Philosophy*. London: J. M. Dent & Sons, 1917.

———. *William James: Writings, 1902–1910*. Edited by Bruce Kuklick. New York: Library of America, 1987.

———. *The Will to Believe and Other Essays in Popular Philosophy*. Edited by Frederick H. Burkhardt. Cambridge, Mass.: Harvard University Press, 1979.

Kaplan, Amy. *The Social Construction of American Realism*. Chicago: University of Chicago Press, 1988.

Kasson, John F. *Amusing the Million: Coney Island at the Turn of the Century*. New York: Hill & Wang, 1978.

Keniston, Kenneth. "Youth as a Stage of Life." In *Readings in Child Development*, edited by Harry Munsinger. New York: Holt, Rinehart & Winston, 1975.

Kern, Stephen. *The Culture of Time and Space, 1880–1918*. Cambridge, Mass.: Harvard University Press, 1983.

Klug, M. A. "Horns of Manichaeus: The Conflict of Art and Experience in *The Great Gatsby* and *The Sun Also Rises*." *Essays in Literature* 12 (Spring 1985): 111–23.

Krutch, Joseph Wood. *The Modern Temper.* New York: Harcourt Brace, 1929.

Kuehl, John, and Jackson R. Bryer, eds. *Dear Scott/Dear Max: The Fitzgerald-Perkins Correspondence.* New York: Charles Scribner's Sons, 1971.

Lears, T. J. Jackson. *No Place of Grace.* Chicago: University of Chicago Press, 1994.

Levin, Harry. *Memories of the Moderns.* New York: New Directions, 1980.

Levinson, Henry Samuel. *Santayana, Pragmatism, and the Spiritual Life.* Chapel Hill: University of North Carolina Press, 1992.

Le Vot, André. *F. Scott Fitzgerald.* Garden City: Doubleday, 1983.

Lewis, Sinclair. *Babbitt.* 1922. Reprint. New York: Signet, 1980.

Lippmann, Walter. *A Preface to Morals.* New York: Macmillan, 1929.

———. *Drift and Mastery: An Attempt to Diagnose the Current Unrest.* New York: Mitchell Kennerly, 1914.

———. *Public Opinion.* New York: Macmillan, 1922.

Lockridge, Ernest H., ed. *Twentieth Century Interpretations of "The Great Gatsby."* Englewood Cliffs: Prentice-Hall, 1968.

Long, Robert Emmet. *The Achieving of "The Great Gatsby."* Lewisburg: Bucknell University Press, 1979.

Lynd, Robert S., and Helen Merrell Lynd. *Middletown: A Study of Modern American Culture.* New York: Harcourt Brace, 1929.

Mellow, James R. *Invented Lives.* Boston: Houghton Mifflin, 1984.

Mencken, H. L. *The Impossible H. L. Mencken: A Selection of His Best Newspaper Stories.* Edited by Marion Elizabeth Rodgers. New York: Anchor, 1991.

———. *A Mencken Chrestomathy.* New York: Vintage, 1982.

———. *My Life as Author and Editor.* Edited by Jonathan Yardley. New York: Vintage, 1995.

——. *A Second Mencken Chrestomathy.* Edited by Terry Teachout. New York: Alfred A. Knopf, 1995.

Merz, Charles. *The Great American Band Wagon.* New York: Literary Guild, 1928.

Meyers, Jeffrey. *Edmund Wilson.* Boston: Houghton Mifflin, 1995.

Ogren, Kathy J. *The Jazz Revolution: Twenties America and the Meaning of Jazz.* New York: Oxford University Press, 1989.

Olian, JoAnn. *Authentic French Fashions of the Twenties.* New York: Dover, 1990.

Oppenheim, Janet. *Shattered Nerves.* New York: Oxford University Press, 1991.

Paulson, Ronald. *Hogarth: His Life, Art, and Times.* New Haven: Yale University Press, 1974.

Perrett, Geoffrey. *America in the Twenties.* New York: Touchstone, 1982.

Petry, Alice Hall. *Fitzgerald's Craft of Short Fiction.* Tuscaloosa: University of Alabama Press, 1989.

Prigozy, Ruth. " 'Poor Butterfly': F. Scott Fitzgerald and Popular Music." *Prospects* 2 (1976): 41–67.

Reynolds, Michael. *Hemingway: The American Homecoming.* Cambridge: Blackwell, 1992.

Royce, Josiah. *The Basic Writings of Josiah Royce.* Edited by John J. McDermott. 2 vols. Chicago: University of Chicago Press, 1969.

——. *William James and Other Essays on the Philosophy of Life.* New York: Macmillan, 1911.

——. *The World and the Individual: Second Series.* New York: Dover, 1901.

Santayana, George. *Character and Opinion in the United States.* 1920. Reprint. New York: Doubleday Anchor, 1956.

————. *The Life of Reason.* New York: Charles Scribner's Sons, 1905.

————. *Santayana on America.* Edited by Richard Colton Lyon. New York: Harcourt, Brace & World, 1968.

Scofield, Martin. *T. S. Eliot: The Poems.* Cambridge: Cambridge University Press, 1988.

Sigg, Eric. *The American T. S. Eliot.* Cambridge: Cambridge University Press, 1989.

Sklar, Robert. *F. Scott Fitzgerald: The Last Laocoon.* New York: Oxford University Press, 1967.

Smith, John E. *The Spirit of American Philosophy.* New York: Oxford University Press, 1963.

Smith, Page. *Redeeming the Time.* New York: McGraw-Hill, 1987.

Stavola, Thomas J. *Scott Fitzgerald: Crisis in an American Identity.* London: Vision Press, 1979.

Stearns, Harold, ed. *Civilization in the United States.* New York: Harcourt Brace, 1922.

Steel, Ronald. *Walter Lippmann and the American Century.* Boston: Little, Brown, 1980.

Stern, Milton R. *The Golden Moment.* Urbana: University of Illinois Press, 1970.

Stuhr, John J., ed. *Classical American Philosophy.* New York: Oxford University Press, 1987.

Tocqueville, Alexis de. *Democracy in America.* Edited by J. P. Mayer. New York: Anchor Books, 1969.

Trilling, Lionel. *The Liberal Imagination.* New York: Viking, 1950.

Twentieth Century Advertising and the Economy of Abundance. Advertising Age (April 30, 1980). [Fiftieth anniversary edition]

Weinstein, Arnold. "Fiction as Greatness: The Case of Gatsby." *Novel* 19 (Fall 1985): 22–38.

Wharton, Edith. *The Age of Innocence.* 1920. Reprint. New York: Collier, 1987.

————. "A Backward Glance." *Edith Wharton: Novellas and Other Writings.* New York: Library of America, 1990.

White, Morton. *Pragmatism and the American Mind.* New York: Oxford University Press, 1973.

Whitman, Cedric. *Homer and the Heroic Tradition.* New York: W. W. Norton, 1958.

Whitman, Robert. *Shaw and the Play of Ideas.* Ithaca: Cornell University Press, 1977.

Wilson, Edmund. *The American Earthquake: A Documentary of the Twenties and Thirties.* New York: Farrar, Straus & Giroux, 1958.

————. *The Shores of Light: A Literary Chronicle of the Twenties and Thirties.* New York: Farrar, Straus & Young, 1952.

————. *The Twenties.* Edited by Leon Edel. New York: Farrar, Straus & Giroux, 1975.

————, ed. *The Crack-Up.* New York: New Directions, 1945.

INDEX

Advertising Age, 56
The Age of Innocence, 64
The American Scene, 100
American Sketch, 94
Arendt, Hannah, 34, 113–14, 118–19
Auden, W. H., 114
Austen, Jane, 73–74

Babbitt, 60, 103, 206 (n. 18)
Babbitt, Irving, 144
"Babylon Revisited," 1, 197
Baltimore Evening Sun, 29
Barzun, Jacques, 29, 65, 203 (n. 13)
"Bernice Bobs Her Hair," 24, 74
Bruccoli, Matthew J., 23, 91

Chambers, John B., 202 (n. 4)
Civilization in the United States, 30, 33
Collier's, 140
The Culture of Time and Space, 1880–1918, 7

The Dance of Life, 86

Depew, Chauncey M., 122–23

Dewey, John, 29; the American scene, 36; arts and sciences, 40–41; community, 84, 93; moral decision, 198, 199; "news," 191; social change, 64

Dial, 30

"The Diamond As Big as the Ritz," 1, 45, 91

"Don't Tell Me What You Dreamed Last Night," 22

Doyle, Sir Arthur Conan, 47–49, 107, 205 (n. 6)

Drift and Mastery, 214 (n. 22)

Dryden, John, 128

The Dyer's Hand, 114

Eliot, T. S., 23, 188

Ellis, Havelock, 86–87

"The Freshest Boy," 116

Freud, Sigmund, 122

Genesis, 45

The Golden Bough, 65

The Golden Moment, 202 (n. 4)

"The Great Community," 93

Harper's Magazine, 94

"Head and Shoulders," 4

Hemingway, Ernest, 54, 83

Hogarth, William, 66

Homer, 129

Hopalong Cassidy, 131

"How Shall We Decorate Our Car?" 53

The Human Condition, 113–14

Hynes, Samuel, 146

"The Ice Palace," 36, 115

"Individual Experience and Social Experience," 156

The Interpretation of Dreams, 22

James, Henry, 93, 94, 100
James, William, 4, 28–42; austerity, 145; community, 84; consciousness, 42, 171; cultural ideas, 137–38; heroism, 116–17; indifference, 152–54; literature, 31–32; love, 159; magazines, 112–13, 138–39; metropolis, 34–35; moral decision, 171–72, 174; moral energies, 116–18; nervous energies, 142–43; order, 198; religion, 46–47; reputation, 4, 29–30; social change, 42; vitality and lethargy, 15–16, 115–16; will, 15–16, 164, 195–97

Keats, John, 111
Keller, Arthur, 47
Kern, Stephen, 7
Krutch, Joseph Wood, 96–97

Levin, Harry, 14, 205–6 (n. 10)
Le Vot, André, 209–10 (n. 7)
Lewis, Sinclair, 206 (n. 18)
The Life of Reason, 7
Lippmann, Walter: American scene, 29, 36; arts and sciences, 34; consciousness, 214 (n. 22); democracy, 65, 95–6; "news," 64–65, 136–38, 190; political ideals, 8; "problem of unbelief," 46; recapturing past, 160–61; resentment, 34, 204 (n. 23); social change, 10, 186
Live Stories, 57
"The Love Nest," 126

Madame Bovary, 14
Major Literary Characters: Gatsby, 205 (n. 8)
Mary (musical), 126
"Materialism and Idealism in American Life," 44
"May Day," 74–75
Mencken, H. L.: aristocracy and democracy, 9, 201 (n. 7), 212 (n. 21); arts and sciences, 34; metropolis, 35, 76–77, 208 (n. 15); "news," 190; reputation of William James, 29
Merz, Charles, 94
Middletown, 56–57
Milton, John, 45

Mizner, Addison, 180–81
"The Moral Philosopher and the Moral Life," 31
Motion Picture Magazine, 57

New Republic, 29, 198, 204 (n. 23)
"Nineteen Hundred and Nineteen," 87

"The Offshore Pirate," 168–69, 199
Oppenheim, Janet, 172–73
Outlook, 94

Perkins, Max, 127
The Philosophy of Loyalty, 158
Post, Emily, 89
"Pragmatic America," 29
Pragmatism, 30, 46, 158–59, 215 (n. 4)
A Preface to Morals, 64
Pride and Prejudice, 74
Public Opinion, 29, 64, 136–38, 190
Public Philosophy, 28, 31–2, 34, 41, 65, 71, 93, 115–16, 136, 155–56, 164, 195

Roosevelt, Theodore, 32, 70, 217–18 (n. 25)
Rousseau and Romanticism, 144
Royce, Josiah: community, 85; individualism, 88; loyalty, 6; metropolis, 35–36, 40; moral indifference, 41; provinces, 35–36, 40; romantic love, 156–60

Santayana, George: aristocracy and democracy, 7–8, 95; civilization, 150–51; democracy, 4, 36; idealism and materialism, 12, 44–45, 50, 68; individualism, 70; Jamesian psychology, 30, 142–43; social order, 7
"Satire on False Perspective," 66
Saturday Evening Post, 23, 33, 36, 102
"The Scandal Detectives," 116
"Scenes and Situations," 181–82
"Search for the Public," 84

"The Sensible Thing," 115, 173
Shaw, George Bernard, 115, 117
Sklar, Robert, 103–4
Smith, Page, 81–82
"Sonnets from the Portuguese," 157
Sources of Religious Insight, 156–60
Stearns, Harold E., 33, 130, 204 (n. 17)
Steele, Frederic Dorr, 47
Stern, Milton, 202 (n. 4)
Strand Magazine, 47
A Stroll with William James, 65
"A Study in Scarlet," 48
The Sun Also Rises, 83
"The Swimmers," 115

Telling Tales, 57
Tender is the Night, 36
This Side of Paradise, 111–13
Tilyou, Edward, 141–42
Tocqueville, Alexis de: equality, 124; materialism, 177; restlessness, 99, 186; ruins, 184–85; society, 98
True Story, 57

"The Valley of Fear," 47
Vanity Fair, 23, 53, 61, 102
Vergil, 128–30
Victorianism, 19–20, 33, 34, 80–81, 98–99, 146–47, 157, 181, 186

The Waste Land, 45
Wells, H. G., 19, 91
Wharton, Edith, 64, 186
White, Morton, 34, 36
Whiteman, Paul, 77–78
"Why the Americans Are Often So Restless," 99
Wiles, Frank, 47

William James and Other Essays on the Philosophy of Life, 6
Wilson, Edmund, 77, 186–88, 193, 208 (n. 19)
Wilson, Woodrow, 70, 85–86
The World's Work, 139–40

Yeats, William Butler, 87

ABOUT THE AUTHOR

Ronald Berman is Professor of Literature, University of California at San Diego. He received his bachelor's degree from Harvard University and his master's and doctorate from Yale University. He has served as chairman of the National Endowment for the Humanities (1971–1977). He has received the Medal of the City of New York. His publications include *Henry King and the Seventeenth Century* (1964), *A Reader's Guide to Shakespeare's Plays* (1965), *The Signet Classic Book of Restoration Drama* (1980), *Advertising and Social Change* (1981), *How Television Sees Its Audience* (1987), *Public Policy and the Aesthetic Interest* (with Ralph A. Smith, 1992), and *The Great Gatsby and Modern Times* (1994).